REAL TIME

DAVID F. BELL

Real Time

ACCELERATING NARRATIVE FROM BALZAC TO ZOLA

UNIVERSITY OF ILLINOIS PRESS
URBANA AND CHICAGO

Manufactured in the United States of America
C 5 4 3 2 1

∞ This book is printed on acid-free paper.

Library of Congress Cataloging-in-Publication Data
Bell, David F.
Real time : accelerating narrative from Balzac to Zola /
David F. Bell.
p. cm.
Includes bibliographical references and index.
ISBN 0-252-02872-4 (cloth : alk. paper)
1. French fiction—19th century—History and criticism.
2. Speed in literature. 3. Communication in literature.
4. Balzac, Honoré de, 1799–1850—Criticism and
interpretation. 5. Zola, Emile, 1840–1902—Criticism
and interpretation. 6. Stendhal, 1783–1842—Criticism
and interpretation. 7. Dumas, Alexandre, 1802–1870—
Criticism and interpretation. I. Title.
PQ653.B38 2004
843'.709355—dc21 2003002474

Contents

Acknowledgments

I would like to thank the National Endowment for the Humanities for a generous fellowship that allowed me to do much of the writing of this book during the 1999–2000 academic year. I owe a debt of gratitude as well to the administration of Arts and Sciences at Duke University for allowing me to accept the NEH grant by releasing me from teaching during the fellowship period.

The material that became this book was the topic of many conversations with colleagues both at Duke and elsewhere, and I would like to thank those who reacted with criticism and suggestions as I explained parts of the project to them. Lawrence Schehr has been a constant and careful interlocutor over the years, and his input along the way has been invaluable—not only for this project, but for many others as well. Pierre Saint-Amand, Marcel Hénaff, Lawrence Kritzman, Franc Schuerewegen, Sydney Lévy, Rae Beth Gordon, and Jean-Marc Lévy-Leblond have been extremely supportive, and I thank them for their interest. Pegge Abrams and Sharon Peters never tired of telling me to get on with it—even at the busiest times. My editor at the University of Illinois Press, Bill Regier, whose enthusiasm and intelligence are infectious, gave me much-needed energy to finish the book and get it into print. My profound gratitude to Martine and Sophie for putting up with me during the hard times.

Part of the second chapter of *Real Time* appeared as "Balzac and the Modern City: Mapping Paris in *Old Goriot,*" in *Approaches to Teaching Balzac's "Old Goriot,"* ed. Michal Peled Ginsburg (New York: Modern Language Association of America, 2000), 81–89. An earlier version of parts of the section in the second chapter dealing with Balzac's *Les Chouans* appeared as "Communication: Euphoria, Dysphoria," *SubStance* 26:2 (1997): 81–95, and I thank the University of Wisconsin Press for permission to use this material.

REAL TIME

Introduction

Like all evolutions in social perception and organization, the restructurings that increased the speed of travel and information exchange in nineteenth-century France were complex. To circumscribe them requires identifying textual sources that give insight into how people adapted their daily practices to incorporate the potential for more rapid movement. The analysis I undertake here is not exhaustive: it does not pretend to cover the entire nineteenth century in a descriptive mode meant to encompass the full gamut of elements associated with questions of speed and communication. Instead I will concentrate on an interval that begins at the end of the eighteenth century and covers roughly the first half of the nineteenth century. The texts that will occupy me most, moreover, are novelistic narratives. These are strategic choices. I want to show that there was already a growing sense of speed—in both the movement of people and the conveying of messages—before the extensive development of the railroad in the 1840s and 1850s in France; hence the decision to focus on the first half of the nineteenth century. And if I have not chosen an archival approach to construct my loosely phenomenological description of the effects of speed, this is because I believe that the controlled nature of the novelistic text offers real insight into the way speed and communication were being woven into the fabric of social perception during the period I have studied. Novels highlight the effects of speed in particularly visible ways. Accordingly, I have chosen to organize my argument around a series of key novels written by four of the most acute social observers of their time: Balzac, Stendhal, Dumas, and Zola.

To talk about speed is necessarily to talk about communication—the two are inseparable during the historical period that will be treated here. I would argue that they are inseparable from the start in any analysis of communication seen as the moving of people and messages. Speed has at least two meanings in this context: (1) the raw speed with which messages and people can get from one place to another, and (2) the quickness—as well as the breadth—with which information, once it transits to a destination, is disseminated among the population sharing the information carried by the messages. How fast people and messages get from one place to another but also who shares messages and has access to them—and how quickly—are crucial questions in any approach to communication. As the reader will see in chapter 2, devoted to relays and stagecoaches, for a significant period of time in the eighteenth and nineteenth centuries, messages (in the form of letters) and passengers transited in the same conveyances under the same tariff models based on distances traveled. Moreover, passengers themselves were vectors for the spread of information and messages. As the stagecoach systems in France and England—and in Europe more broadly—improved, the passing of information up and down the line by drivers, mail guards, and passengers became an important function of the overland transportation network. The speed of movement of passengers will be as much at stake in the pages that follow as the speed of message exchanges.

A brief scene in Charles Dickens's novel *Oliver Twist* (serialized between 1837 and 1839) captures quite symptomatically some of the elements characteristic of the convergence between speedy and precise overland travel, on the one hand, and the exchange of messages and information, on the other. Bill Sikes flees London after having beaten Nancy to death. Starved for information about whether the murder has been discovered and the pursuit of the culprit organized, he stumbles onto the passage of the mail coach in the small village of Hatfield: "He almost knew what was to come; but he crossed over, and listened" (427). What is to come in the scene is none other than the dissemination of the news concerning the murder he has committed. Sikes (almost) knows that the mail coach brings the news and that the passengers and the employees all have the same desire to be the first to announce it—yet he is drawn into the process almost magnetically. Within seconds he hears what he most fears:

> "Anything new up in town, Ben?" asked the gamekeeper, drawing back to the window-shutters, the better to admire the horses.
>
> "No, nothing that I knows on," replied the man, pulling on his gloves. "Corn's up a little. I heerd talk of a murder, too, down Spitalfields way, but I don't reckon much upon it."

> "Oh, that's quite true," said a gentleman inside, who was looking out of the window. "And a dreadful murder it was." (427)

In an extraordinarily telling manner, commodity market news (the price of corn) and what the French call *faits divers* (news briefs about accidents, murders, and local events—in this case, the murder of Nancy) are woven together. The increased speed of communication that will be at the heart of my analysis makes the stock and commodity markets a national issue and local disasters a national interest.[1] Bill Sikes encounters immediate confirmation that the tidings of his deed are out on the roads, as it were (before the historical periods when they would be "on the wires" or "on the air"). Just hours after the murder was committed he has become a widely hunted man. The pursuit organized by the quick dissemination of information about the crime and about Sikes himself makes his flight a hopeless prospect and quickly forces him back to London, where he believes he has a better chance to hide than he does in any village along the stagecoach line.

There is more to the scene, however. Dickens makes it amply clear that the mail coach guard is in a hurry and is irritated by a delay that seems to have become chronic at the Hatfield stop: "Now, look alive in there, will you. Damn that 'ere bag, it warn't ready night afore last; this won't do, you know!" (427). After the travelers and the employees exchange the news about the murder, the driver becomes even more agitated, ultimately cutting off the conversation:

> "Damn that 'ere bag," said the guard; "are you going to sleep in there?"
> "Coming!" cried the office keeper, running out.
> "Coming," growled the guard. "Ah, and so's the young 'ooman of property that's going to take a fancy to me, but I don't know when. Here, give hold. All ri—ght!"
> The horn sounded a few cheerful notes, and the coach was gone. (427)

The haste of the postal guard and the rapidity with which the office keeper comes running out of the relay station carrying the object of contention are at the heart of my concerns. The hectic pace vividly highlights expectations about being on time. These expectations clearly affect the behavior of those connected with the mail, be they passengers or employees. Impatience and tensions run high, and the passengers and employees speak in a language of telegraphic brevity, at least until the climactic and more sustained irony of the mail guard's last remark. Time is short, movements need to be accomplished quickly, embellishments are out of place.

As striking as the results of the reorganization of the overland travel infrastructure during the first half of the nineteenth century may appear to the present-day reader willing to devote some attention to them, the conception and building of a rather complete optical telegraph network in France during the same period may be even more remarkable for the changes it wrought in the domain of communication. Well before the perfecting of the technological innovations necessary for the creation of an electrical telegraph network, the French had installed the best semaphore telegraph network in Europe. My third and fourth chapters will explore the motivations behind its construction and the technologies of its functioning, but it is important to provide here at least an introductory taste of the cultural visibility and influence of this system for those who lived during the period in question. A suggestive entry into the presence of the optical telegraph system in the cultural landscape of France in the first half of the nineteenth century can be provided by recalling the beginning of the fourth book of the first part of Victor Hugo's *Quatrevingt-treize.*[2] That passage in the novel recounts the landing in Brittany of the marquis de Lantenac, after a naval battle that results in the disastrous sinking of the ship in which he is traveling. Saved from drowning, Lantenac makes his way to shore and is lulled into a reflective mood by the sunset on the coastal landscape. Shortly thereafter, he is startled by what is at first an inexplicable phenomenon:

> Suddenly, he stood up.
>
> His attention had been abruptly awakened. He looked toward the horizon. Something caused him to focus with particular intensity.
>
> He was looking at the Cormeray bell tower, which was in front of him at the far end of the plain. Something inexplicable and extraordinary was indeed happening in this bell tower.
>
> The silhouette of the tower was in clear relief; one could see it topped off by its pyramid-shaped roof, and, between the tower and the pyramid, the belfry containing the bell. The belfry was square, open, with no panels to protect against the wind, visible on all four sides, a typical Breton bell tower.
>
> But the belfry seemed alternately to open and close; at regular intervals, its high window was completely white, then completely black; one could see the sky through the openings, and then one could not see it; clarity was followed by obscurity; and the opening and closing of the window happened in succession from one second to the next with the regularity of a hammer striking an anvil.
>
> The old man [Lantenac disguised] could see the Cormeray bell tower in front of him, at a distance of about two leagues.[3]

As Lantenac scans the horizon from his elevated position, he can see eight additional bell towers, and they are all doing the same thing. After a moment's reflection, he realizes that he is seeing an alarm broadcast using the bells in the towers, which are oscillating back and forth as they ring and are thus functioning like shutters, alternately obscuring and revealing the sunlight that passes through the open windows in the belfry. From Lantenac's distant observation point, however, the ocean breeze prevents the sound from reaching him and transforms the phenomenon into a purely visual one. The way Hugo describes this scene would quite simply have been impossible without the extensive exposure he had to the optical telegraph, a technology that visually marked the French countryside during the first half of the nineteenth century. The very symbols of the secularization of France imposed by the Revolution and its aftermath were disaffected churches that had been turned to other uses. In particular, the towers of such edifices had more than occasionally been transformed into semaphore telegraph broadcasters. The optical telegraph required that the signaling mechanisms be installed on a promontory, a characteristic often possessed by churches, which had systematically been erected on higher ground for symbolic purposes. The towers of disaffected churches made ideal telegraph repeating stations, and Hugo is absolutely cognizant of this fact when he imagines this scene.[4]

In the passage from *Quatrevingt-treize* quoted above, Hugo the visionary novelist creates a strangely anachronistic warping, imposing on a scene ostensibly set in 1793 (the very year during which the main part of the work was done on the first lengthy optical telegraph line between Paris and Lille) a fictional structure that could only be imagined by an author who had grown up seeing the repeating towers of the semaphore telegraph network in operation—and who remembered that spectacle while composing the novel in 1874. The communication among the bell towers that Lantenac perceives becomes in the author's fantasy a visual code, passed along from promontory to promontory, in a configuration that is functionally equivalent to the operation of the optical telegraph. Although the French optical telegraph network ultimately did not use a shutter configuration, the Danish one did. A code mobilizing shutter positions was thus a competing technology during the period of operation of the old optical telegraph system in France.[5] Hugo transforms the bell towers into optical devices using sunlight and shutters (the bells themselves), unconsciously producing the semblance of a semaphore code when the bells oscillate in their towers. Just as observers of the optical telegraph stations could speculate on the contents of the messages passed visibly up and down the line, messages that were for the most part inscrutable, so also Lantenac tries to interpret the meaning of the coded signals he perceives. The full significance of this passage in *Quatrevingt-treize* unfolds only when a certain cultural and technological history can allow us to understand it.[6]

Technologies of speed and communication and their impact on French culture are thus at the core of my discussion. A word about the notion of technology is therefore in order. In particular, the relation between science and technology and the history of that relation have an impact on the argument set forth here. If at least part of the domain of communication has become a "science" in our contemporary world and can be summed up in a series of algorithms (of which perhaps those proposed by Shannon and Weaver in *Mathematical Theory of Communication* are the most famous historically speaking), the development of this field of reflection during the first half of the nineteenth century would seem to belong resolutely to the realm of technology. What is the relation between science and technology? The complexities of this question go back to the founding moments of modern science with Galileo and Newton, when the overwhelming and indisputable theoretical successes of classical mechanics made that discipline the unavoidable model of what it actually meant to be scientific in one's approach to the world. To be scientific required that one create a set of abstract equations that conjoined seemingly diverse sets of natural phenomena (things as far removed from one another in common experience, for example, as the movement of celestial bodies and the movement of a pendulum). Classical mechanics gave such disparate phenomena a striking coherence based on a set of laws that could be summarized in a series of articulated equations. Historians of science and scientists themselves would now say, of course, that there is not one science, not a single model for scientific activity, but a plurality of sciences; in other words, scientific method is, in reality, a group of diverse methods. It would be impossible to unite them by means of a simplified set of abstract principles, which one could use to eliminate scientific pretenders flawlessly in each case. Nevertheless, the monolithic view of science defined as an activity of abstraction characterized by the methods of Newtonian mechanics remains a powerful temptation. The "myth" of classical mechanics still holds sway over the minds of many specialists and nonspecialists alike. Interactions with natural phenomena that do not quite measure up to the abstracting powers of classical mechanics are somehow less scientific; they are "applications"; they are "technologies"; they fall under the purview of "engineers," not of scientists. Classical mechanics set the stage for contrasting "formal" science with less abstract, more circumstantial encounters with natural phenomena.

In a concise but provocative essay entitled "Le Pouvoir des concepts," Isabelle Stengers shows how in the *Encyclopédie,* to take a classic example, Enlightenment thinkers were already at work fending off the abstract model of science that Newtonian mechanics had made into such a powerful intellectual attraction (almost as if the *force d'attraction* at the heart of Newtonian theory referred simultaneously to a sort of core fascination with the theory itself and its methods). Stengers analyzes the encyclopedia entry devoted to the term *chymie,* written by the chemist and medical doctor Venel, and shows how it develops a powerful oppositional position against the Newtonian paradigm. The Stengers argument can perhaps better situate a cultural and literary approach to speed and communication in the nineteenth century in France that revalorizes technology, or what one might call an approach to phenomena that gives a proper place to complexity and circumstances. In his entry on *chymie,* Venel confronts immediately and explicitly the problem of whether chemistry can be conceived as a science in the form provided by the model of Newtonian mechanics. His answer is no, because, as he claims, the chemist will never be able to avoid the long and arduous apprenticeship, "which gives him a discerning eye," as Stengers puts it, "the faculty for interpreting indices, for understanding the multiple circumstances that were at work in any given transformation and the capacity to succeed in reproducing the circumstances that allow given reactions to take place" (42). Chemistry is a passion, a real engagement of the body in the circumstances that produce the various reactions studied. The notion of engagement suggests that procedures creating distance—in other words, instruments and abstractions that remove the chemist from the context in which reactions take place—are to be decried. The work of the chemist is, very precisely, an art of the circumstance, which renders the step toward abstraction in each case enormously complex.

Such declarations should not be dismissed as ridiculous or outmoded—they represent the real state of the profession of the chemist and of the medical doctor at the time when Venel, who was both, composed his article in the mid-eighteenth century. Nothing can spare the chemist or the doctor the arduous work of interpreting circumstances. But Stengers reminds us as well that the position taken by Venel contains an added political charge beyond its methodological commentary:

> For Diderot and Venel, the resistance encountered by those who want to submit chemistry to the model of classical mechanics is the resistance that the real activity of matter creates—blocking the pretension of those who refuse to get their hands dirty. The power of the scientific concept, which allows one to abstract from the circumstances, to submit the set of all phenomena to a generalizing judgment, corresponds to the power that the small number of those who "reflect" wield over the mass of those who "act," as Diderot puts it. The model of classical mechanics is thus

> one of an elitist science that ignores what it cannot understand and holds all those who "do not know" what the right questions are in contempt, that is, all those who are recognized as incapable of producing something that would have the status of a "scientific fact." (43)

Clearly, then, the *Encyclopédie* reflects here and elsewhere the difference between those who accept the complexities of circumstances and those who prefer abstraction, between those who engage with the convoluted imbrication of natural phenomena in their own everyday practices and those who choose to remain in the abstract world of theory. There is, among other things, a power struggle at the heart of these distinctions: the power of the Newtonians would be the result of an attempt to disqualify the great mass of the rest of us, who are inevitably engaged in the teeming circumstances of a life defined precisely by a level of complexity that defies abstraction. Newtonian theory may miraculously have allowed certain researchers to define a limited set of phenomena in a new and astoundingly effective way; it may have permitted a kind of prediction unheard of previously, but it has no legislative validity to prescribe how the other 99 percent of natural and cultural phenomena can and should be approached.

Chemistry is an excellent test case for Stengers, because it is a domain that became "scientific" only during the nineteenth century, and it became so largely as the result of industrial and technological advances. Practices used by artisans to extract raw materials end up producing materials that are never quite the same, that always differ in concentration and mixture when they are discovered and lifted directly from nature. Such practices gradually gave way during the nineteenth century to the industrialized production of standard, purified, and/or synthesized products that could eventually become the objects of a science of generalities and abstractions resembling modern chemistry, precisely because they were standardized and could therefore be produced in a manner that made them available in the same form to anyone who had industrial access to them.

Stengers's analysis of the problems faced by early chemists can be used to frame some of the issues one deals with when thinking about technologies of communication in France in the nineteenth century. The "science" of communication, which is more or less a mid-twentieth-century development—if one wants to date it from the moment when it matured into a true theoretical domain—was rendered possible and necessary only because of the exponential rate of technological development that increased the speed of communication dramatically in the second half of the nineteenth century and in the first half of the twentieth (railroad, electrical telegraph, telephone, radio, and airplane). The increasing speed in message exchange and in the movement of people required more systematic reflection on the structures of communication, a search for theoretical efficiencies, and eventually the formulation of theoretical approaches that would allow further material advances. The complexity of communication theory, however, derives partly from the fact that it deals not only with the movement of messages but also with the movement of people. Such complexities prevent the immediate formulation of more abstract theoretical perspectives and require an accumulation of technological and sociological experience over time in preparation for a more theoretical view on the problems generated by the various technologies mobilized. Gradual nineteenth- and twentieth-century developments preceded and ultimately gave rise to the possibility of such abstraction: from the reorganization of the stagecoach system to the building of the optical telegraph, from the construction of the railroad and the electrical telegraph to the invention of the telephone and then of wireless communication, which was in turn linked to the development of aviation. In short, at the end of a long series of technological and sociological developments, speed in information exchange and in the movement of people had become a crucial characteristic of the modern world. When that speed radically exceeded the scale of lived rhythms that had marked mankind for countless previous centuries, the time was ripe for a serious attempt at abstraction in this domain.

The corpus of novels available to examine the phenomena of speed and communication in nineteenth-century France is certainly rich. The novels to be examined here provide but a sampling of that richness. From the travel experiences of Doctor Minoret in Balzac's *Ursule Mirouët* to the effortless voyages of Dumas's count of Monte-Cristo, from the impetuosity of the Napoleonic cavalry officer Philippe Bridau in Balzac's *La Rabouilleuse* to Lucien Leuwen's mastery of the English thoroughbred in Stendhal's *Lucien Leuwen,* from the transiting of documents and voyagers in Balzac's *Un Début dans la vie* to the sending and receiving of optical telegraph messages in both *Lucien Leuwen* and *Le Comte de Monte-Cristo:* in this era preceding the railroads, people and messages were moving more quickly and precisely than ever before or than might be imagined by today's casual reader. The novels I will examine in detail are filled with such traces, but the motivation behind the constitution of the literary corpus I will exploit in my argument runs deeper. Assuredly, questions dealing with transportation and transmission of messages in France in the first half of the nineteenth century are reflected in the novels analyzed in the historian's sense. One could treat the novels as documents, as pieces of an archive. And I have done this in part. I will make a stronger claim, however, as my discussion unfolds: the novels I have chosen to analyze are in fact largely structured by implicit and explicit approaches to the problems raised by the organizational changes occurring in the domain of travel and communication. More than themes, these issues become veritable structuring principles.

In chapter 1, for example, it quickly becomes apparent that an understanding of the argument on family relations in Balzac's *Ursule Mirouët* is incomplete if one does not connect the novelist's analysis to the question of roads and stagecoach relays. The novel's structure revolves around Minoret-Levrault's hold on the communicational network around Nemours, which gives him mastery as well of the complex family relations underlying a desperate struggle for an inheritance. In a second novel dealing with provincial relations and a clash over an inheritance, *La Rabouilleuse,* Balzac turns the confrontation between Philippe Bridau and Maxence Gilet into a competition between the cavalry officer and the infantryman, giving this increasingly violent and ultimately mortal quarrel between Napoleonic veterans an unexpected twist that brings speed and maneuvering to the fore.

In chapter 2, I turn to Balzac's *Un Début dans la vie,* a novel that tells the story of the formation of the Restoration bourgeoisie through a description of the education of Oscar Husson. What will interest me most, however, is that the tale describing Oscar's social insertion is framed by two voyages in a local stagecoach, trips that serve as a veritable dissertation on the situation of overland travel after Napoleon. The framing device makes the stagecoach voyage a central element of the text, the place where, as novelistic tradition would have it, the characters encounter each other fortuitously, but also the place where the very development of the bourgeoisie in question is chronicled through the economic rise of Pierrotin, the owner of a stagecoach line. In a reading of *Les Chouans,* the chapter will also take up the importance of military maneuvering on roads, highlighting the relation between movement on roads and the immobility of fortifications and suggesting that one of the crucial characteristics of the republic was its push to "take to the roads," to send the republican army out on the road network to subdue the enemies of the republic. The chapter closes with a reading of *Le Père Goriot* that emphasizes the importance of mapping the new and complex city space, a lesson in topography for Eugène de Rastignac, who learns how certain short circuits bring topographically unrelated neighborhoods of the city into a series of unexpected and instantaneous encounters that reflect a new social organization.

Chapter 3 turns to Stendhal's *Lucien Leuwen* and argues that it is structured as a diptych on speed. The first half of the novel is an extended study of horsemanship and the second half at least partially a treatise on the optical telegraph and the ways in which it redefines the political through a system of rapid message exchanges. Balzac's *Une Ténébreuse affaire* is then treated because, as we shall see, it also deals with prodigious feats of horsemanship—this time accomplished by a woman who ultimately outrides the telegraph, a telegraph commandeered by the very secret policeman, Corentin, who traveled the roads (before policemen began to "ride the rails") in *Les Chouans,* experimenting with movement and secret message exchanges.

Chapter 4 is devoted to Alexandre Dumas's *Le Comte de Monte-Cristo* and argues that the principal character in the novel is something like the ultimate expert on speed of the late 1830s and early 1840s, both in his own movements on water and on land and in his knowledge of message systems in France.

I conclude with a treatment of Zola's *La Bête humaine,* which allows me to look briefly at one of the culmination points in the development of the structures and expectations set up by rapid stagecoach travel and the optical telegraph, namely, the railroad. If the railroad ultimately introduced a break in evolutionary trends because of the quantum leap in speed that it allowed, I would also argue that it built on organizational structures and demands that were created well before its construction began in earnest. In my conclusion, I will make a connection between railroad speed and transformed visual perception, marking certain continuities that exist with elements that preceded the railroad.

The readings undertaken here are a hybrid exercise, proposing a movement back and forth between history and novelistic fiction with the intention of showing to what extent the novelistic projects of Balzac, Stendhal, Dumas, and Zola are immersed in a certain technological history and evolution. If it is indeed true that one can analyze literature from a certain perspective as communication—whatever the historical period might be—it may also be said that the novels analyzed here are immersed with a rare intensity in a veritable communicational transmutation, restructuring the expectations of fictional characters in ways that can help us gauge the importance of these changes within the society in which the novels were written. The increased speed of the movement of both people and messages was destined to make of communication an increasingly important notion, one that would finally spawn a complex science of communication in the twentieth century.

1 Webs: Genealogies, Roads, Streets (Balzac)

In Balzac's *Ursule Mirouët,* everyone is on the move. In the first scene, the *maître de poste* (postmaster) in Nemours, Minoret-Levrault, awaits the arrival of a coach carrying his son, Désiré, who is returning home to Nemours from Paris after completing his law studies. Another Minoret, Doctor Minoret, who comes to Nemours to retire after a very long absence from the town and whose return will provoke the struggle for his inheritance that is the main narrative line of the novel, thinks nothing of jumping into a coach and traveling substantial distances to treat sick patients in provincial towns well outside Paris during the period when his medical practice is based in the capital. Moreover, in the last part of the novel, as the struggle is finally engaged to right the injustice that occurs after Doctor Minoret's death when his estate is stolen from its rightful heir, a system of "shuttle diplomacy" between key characters in Nemours and the *procureur du roi* (prosecutor) in Fontainebleau begins. It ends only with a catastrophic accident on the very road that permits almost frenetic commuting between the two towns. What is the significance of all this traveling? What is its relation to the other themes that are developed in the novel? Answers to these questions will lead us first toward the issue of collateral relations and then toward a discussion of how such relations are connected to questions of transportation and speed of movement on roads. In a way that will become clear shortly, the issue of family relations and the networks they create is superimposed on the pattern of exchange networks created by the road system that is such an integral part of the novel. Family relations in Balzac's novel cannot be understood without reference to road networks. The notion of transport is perhaps the best way to try to understand what provincial families have become during the Restoration Balzac so constantly attempts to portray.

Ursule Mirouët is a novel about collateral relations. The term "collateral" exists in both English and French, although its usage is not quite the same in the two languages. In particular, *les collatéraux* in its substantive form in French refers to all those members of a family who descend from a common ancestor without descending directly from each other, in particular, various degrees of cousins. Balzac uses the term in the novel in order to explore what he considers to be a veritable genealogical and social problem and thus to create one of those characteristic moments of sociological reflection that are dispersed so strategically throughout the series of novels that make up *La Comédie humaine.* If one wanted to be slightly ironic in characterizing the novel, it could be said that the story deals with "collateral damage," a play on an expression in English using the term. In this case, however, at stake is not damage caused to people or things near a military target but the damage, both moral and material, caused by the collaterals themselves, that is, the cousins in the Minoret-Levrault family clustered about the provincial town of Nemours.

It would be useful first to set the stage for Balzac's remarks on genealogy in this novel of family relations. Placed at the beginning of "Scènes de la vie de province," *Ursule Mirouët* opens with a scene whose main character is Minoret-Levrault, mentioned above. This imposing personage is sitting at the end of the bridge leading into Nemours and fretting about the fact that the coach carrying his son home from Paris is late. He is certainly well placed as *maître de poste* to know that this delay could mean the coach has had an accident in which his son has been injured: "The stagecoach bringing his only son usually arrived in Nemours at around five o'clock in the morning, and the clock had just struck nine! What was the cause of such a delay? Had the coach tipped over? Was Désiré still alive? Perhaps only his leg was broken?"[1] The reader later learns that the delay was caused when one of the coach's wheels lost its steel rim—an incident that could well have resulted in a broken wheel and a serious accident: "The rim of one of the rear wheels came off between Essonne and Ponthierry. But there was no accident. On the way up the hill, Cabirolle luckily realized what had happened" (3:775). As we shall see, Minoret-Levrault's anticipation of an accident opens a narrative that will come to a close with the actual occurrence of the imagined catastrophe—in the very place where Minoret-Levrault is sitting when the novel opens and with the very effect feared from the outset: Désiré will be crushed when a coach rolls over him, resulting in his death. Minoret-Levrault's ruminations are more than narrative foreshadowing, however. They reflect a real state of affairs. Although conditions of road travel in 1829, when the novel begins, had considerably improved in the course of the preceding fifty years, serious material problems remained. The roads themselves, for example, were of varied quality and susceptible to severe damage during seasons of bad weather. The typical journey included considerable discomfort on the part of the traveler, as the conveyance—coach, cart, or hybrid of the two—negotiated rocky surfaces, washed-out roads, and potholes of all sorts. "Friction wore out vehicles as well as men. At any moment a trip could be interrupted by a broken axle, a broken carriage that had to be repaired," as Christophe Studeny puts it (41). Difficult roads interacted with fragile equipment to make the risk of accident ever present for the coach rider. Minoret-Levrault cannot ignore the risks of the situation.

Another element comes into play to suggest the origin of Minoret-Levrault's behavior at the beginning of the novel—even if it is not made absolutely explicit by the narrator. If the reader tries to understand exactly why Minoret-Levrault is so worried by the delay in the coach's arrival, an easy presupposition quickly becomes problematic. A modern reader might assume without reflection that the delay was normal. After all, stagecoaches were subject to the vagaries of a quite imperfect road system. How could the schedules for the circulation of coaches have been exact enough to warrant the behavior displayed? Historians of the development of the railroad system have shown how trains synchronized national time zones and set up expectations about the regularity of schedules (the international agreement establishing Greenwich Mean Time, for example, went into effect in 1883). But less has been said about these issues in the period preceding the railroad. Balzac's scene shows us that in 1829, when the novel opens, the organization of the coach system had reached a point where travelers and townspeople had a certain degree of confidence in coach service schedules. There was an expectation of precision, despite the imperfections of the land transportation system.[2] Time could be kept fairly accurately based on the arrivals and departures of the vehicles in question. The reader should be reminded that after Turgot took the coach and the road systems in hand in 1775, a series of improvements, both in the construction of the coaches themselves and in the upkeep of the roads they used, helped regularize and speed up service, especially between important towns.[3] A scene such as the one recounted in the first pages of *Ursule Mirouët* doubtless would not have been imaginable fifty years earlier, but by 1829, the *maître de poste,* himself partial creator of the schedules used for arrivals and departures, has certain expectations about the exactness of the transportation service in which he works.

The structure of the transportation network, barely suggested in this first scene in the novel, is closely linked to the question of family relations. This linkage needs to be analyzed if one is to grasp the originality of the description Balzac constructs in *Ursule Mirouët.* Minoret-Levrault's wait is interrupted by his cousin, Mme. Massin, who arrives on the scene to tell him that their uncle, Doctor Minoret, has gone to mass with Ursule Mirouët. Minoret-Levrault and Mme. Massin are soon joined by another character, the *percepteur des contributions* (tax collector) in Nemours, M. Crémière. Then Massin-Levrault Junior, Mme. Massin's husband and a law clerk in the town, comes along as well. Massin-Levrault Junior is accompanied by M. Crémière's wife. It would be hard to imagine a reader who at this point in the story would not be completely confused by the rapidly assembled group of characters, whose names arrive in a staccato sequence with little help provided by the narrator to understand the group's significance. No common elements seem to join them together. The first indication of what might relate these people to one another is given in the following remark made by the narrator: "Almost all of the relations [*collatéraux*] of old Doctor Minoret were together on the square" (3:780). What we have here, then, is the group of those who are sufficiently related to the doctor to have some interest in the disposition of his inheritance, the cousins, both distant and more directly connected to him. That the doctor has attended mass is a considerable surprise and a source of deep concern for all his collaterals in Nemours. It introduces a new element, another calculation into the plans of the relatives, who believed until now that they had determined a strategy for gaining control of the doctor's fortune. Does the fact that the doctor has attended mass mean that he is contemplating a gift to the Catholic Church or that he has definitively chosen the pious Ursule as his sole heir? The collaterals assembled in the street in Nemours are startled in part, moreover, because the doctor's reputation as a Voltairean makes his presence at a Catholic mass quite unexpected. This first scene of the novel informs the reader of the situation that organizes the story: upon the retirement of Doctor Minoret to Nemours, his distant relatives have done everything possible to be written into his will, while the doctor has done everything possible to divert his inheritance almost exclusively toward his ward, Ursule.[4]

Balzac does not stop there in his development of the first narrative sequence, however. The notion of "collaterals" immediately gives rise to more complex and general remarks about the composition of provincial society in the town of Nemours. As is often the case in *La Comédie humaine,* society in Nemours is divided between a nobility, few and rather powerless in this instance, and a bourgeoisie that is the real source of political and economic energy in the town. The bourgeois majority, with its peculiar genealogical structure, is what really attracts Balzac's attention. The members of the bourgeoisie in question are largely the descendants of a very small number of families—four to be exact. Since the reign of Louis XI, the main bourgeois clusters in the region have all originated from the Minoret, Massin, Levrault, and Crémière groups. The composition of the Nemours bourgeoisie thus has the form of an algebra with four variables giving rise to a series of endless permutations:

> Under Louis XIII, these four families were already producing offspring named Massin-Crémière, Levrault-Massin, Massin-Minoret, Minoret-Minoret, Crémière-Levrault, Levrault-Minoret-Massin, Massin-Levrault, Minoret-Massin, Massin-Massin, Crémière-Massin, assorted with various and sundry "juniors" and "eldest," with Crémière-François, Levrault-Jacques, Jean-Minoret. It was enough to drive the people's Father Anselme mad, if indeed the people ever needed a genealogist.[5] The variations of this domestic kaleidoscope made up of four elements were further complicated by births and marriages such that the genealogical tree of the bourgeois in Nemours would have stumped the Benedictines of the Gotha Almanac themselves, despite the atomistic science they employed to lay out the zigzags of German family alliances.[6] (3:782)

In short, these four families have occupied all points of this social space and closed it off from others, as Claudie Bernard has argued in her article on family dynamics in *Ursule Mirouët:* "Like so many tentacles, bourgeois dynasties have invaded the social space. They reign supreme in the city, have established themselves in the outlying towns—and even in Paris" (182).

This situation is not confined to Nemours. In fact, it characterizes social organization throughout France, and even throughout Europe in the period, if Balzac is to be believed: "In whatever countries you may go, the names may change, but you will find the same thing" (3:783). He even goes so far as to invent a neologism to characterize the situation he is describing—"cognomonisme."[7] Ironically, then, genealogy is necessarily called upon to play a crucial role in a society that was in many ways supposed to have been a post-genealogical society. Under the *ancien régime,* one had to prove that one belonged to a noble family in order to justify the right to enjoy what were called the "privileges" of the nobility. Thus official genealogists had a fundamental task: they had to decide which branches were legitimate, which branches to cut off, which branches were properly grafted to the family tree, which grafts could not be allowed to take. If the Revolution was supposed to have put an end to this system and to have replaced it by an order of merit, Balzac shows us that this was far from being the case. Genealogy becomes once again a principal structuring technique in postrevolutionary bourgeois society, but simultaneously it has become considerably more complex, more hidden and deceptive. It now has to deal with botanical forms that open onto the possibility of confusion, of something one might ultimately call a generalized social conspiracy. The society of collaterals is almost the equivalent of a secret society. Developing the botanical metaphor, Balzac prefers the image of a system of interwoven roots that radiate outward in complex directions. We are not very far from the notion of radiating influence that Zola applies to his description of the Rougon-Macquart family during the Second Empire, imagined as something like vectors of infection that spread out and invade all sectors of the social structure. The metaphor is no longer the noble image of the tree that grows upward with visible and clear branching in all its majesty, but rather an image describing a system of roots that propagates in a hidden and inextricably scrambled progression. Such a system allows unexpected intersections, unpredictable twists and grafts.

Bernard has argued that Balzac's analysis ultimately defines a proletariat of collateral relations whose contours are rendered visible precisely through the question of money and fortune, that is, through the necessity of a vigorous struggle for social survival that always has to do with economic exchange and inheritance patterns: "The 'proletarian' is defined by . . . his descendants, *proles,* more numerous than those of the elite. His proliferating bloodline threatens society with a revolution that will be worse than any of the preceding ones" (183). Because the cousins are always those who are either cut off from an inheritance or receive very little of it, they are forced to fend for themselves, to make their fortunes through socially stressful confrontations with all the other cousins. But this "melting pot" effect of the collaterals goes further. The genealogies of both the nobility and the bourgeoisie are destined to come together, to be inextricably tangled—yet another aspect of the problem that promises political and social upheavals. If, as the biblical passages quoted by Balzac dealing with the multiplication of populations would have it, two or three families suffice to populate the entire earth in a relatively short period of time, then, "a family can become a nation, and, unhappily, a nation can become simply a single family again" (3:783). One can trace back sufficiently far into the past to show the common origin of all French citizens. And perhaps one need not trace back very far at all, since the law of demographic growth, demographic "irradiation," as Balzac terms it, is a law of exponential progression. The novelist demonstrates this—in the same passage—when he refers to the ancient anecdote concerning the inventor of chess, who reputedly asked for compensation for his invention in the form of a quantity of wheat that would be doubled for each square on the chessboard (3:783). The doubling effect quickly creates an astronomically high number, a quantity of wheat that no one could assemble. The demographic increase in the number of collaterals is a comparable phenomenon. Not only do the collaterals confront one another as hungry have-nots, they accomplish the last act in a process of social mixture that brings an end to the distinction between nobility and bourgeoisie. Small wonder that this phenomenon is seen by Balzac as a threat to social stability. The Revolution would thus be conceived as something like the moment when an attempt was made to transform the long history of class mixture into the realization of a classless society, one that simply recognized the demographic facts. Unfortunately, however, this realization remained incomplete, and the nineteenth century inherited the problems left over after that failed recognition, Balzac suggests.

The distribution of the collaterals, viewed as a system of proliferating roots, must be seen as a network. Balzac puts it like this: "Filled with the same blood and bearing the same name to complete the similitude, these four loom shuttles [that is, the four bourgeois families at the origin of Nemours society since the reign of Louis XI] had tirelessly woven a human web" (3:783). Or take the following formulation: "The lacework of the nobility [was] encompassed by the lacework of the bourgeoisie" (3:783). The term Balzac uses here, "lacis" in French, designates the network of threads in a tissue that has been sewn or woven, for example, in lacework, but by extension it also means an intertwining system of roads. My brief earlier remarks on the road system after Turgot intersect in a fascinating way with the question of family relations—the two are linked by the notion of the network. We have seen that Minoret-Levrault is the *maître de poste* of Nemours, that is, he occupies a place at the center, on the turntable of the network of roads that situates Nemours in the context of this society of collaterals characteristic of the Restoration. Balzac even shortens Minoret-Levrault's professional title with some regularity, calling him *le maître de Nemours,* "the master of Nemours," rather than *le maître de poste de Nemours,* "the postmaster of Nemours." This abbreviation is highly symptomatic, given the strategic position he holds. Minoret-Levrault is also Doctor Minoret's principal collateral and will eventually become the perpetrator of the theft of his estate after the doctor's death. When Balzac describes Minoret-Levrault, he underlines the character's peasant lineage, calling attention to his girth and his uncouthness ("grand et gros homme"). Despite his central social and strategic position within the superimposed networks of the family and the road system, he has barely been able to separate himself from his rustic origins. Minoret-Levrault need not demonstrate any particularly exceptional qualities, however, in order to thrive—what counts is how he is situated with respect to essential nodes along the network of transportation in this society defined by the circulation of goods and people.[8] Not only do his cousins blanket the region, but the system of coaches he directs does exactly the same thing.

Minoret-Levrault's fortune grows in an almost automatic and exponential fashion and is built on the foundations of his substantial farming in an *ancien régime* agricultural mode: "Despite his visible incapacities, with the help of the Revolution and over a period of thirty-six years he had amassed a fortune that brought him an income of thirty thousand pounds per year—from grazing lands, farmland, and woods. If Minoret was still working, despite his investments in the coach company in Nemours and in the Gâtinais coach company in Paris, it was less out of habit than with a view to establishing a bright future for his only son" (3:772). The *maîtres de poste* who were in charge of coach operations in larger towns on more traveled roads within the highway network of the period naturally became large-scale agricultural producers. They needed fodder to maintain the numerous horses with which they dealt and were led to produce it rather than to buy it. The extension of Minoret-Levrault's activities is thus within the logic of his situation and not necessarily a reflection of his intelligence or innate capacities. He lives during the golden age of *maîtres de poste:* "All the historians of the stagecoach system agree that the Empire, the Restoration, and the July Monarchy were the golden age of the stagecoach," as Henri Cavaillès remarks in his study on French roads since the Middle Ages (222). Of course, not all *maîtres de poste* were as successful as Minoret-Levrault. The juridical texts from the period, the laws that were modified, voted, and applied concerning the organization of the stagecoach transportation system, were especially favorable to *maîtres de poste* in places that were key nodes on the network. This select few so thrived that historians can speak of a "relay aristocracy": "They did not all benefit equally. Out of the 1,400 to 1,500 *maîtres de poste* who ran the relays in France, the majority eked out a meager existence. The large profits went to a small minority. . . . These lucky and privileged few made up a sort of aristocracy of the relay system" (Cavaillès 222–23). The fact that Minoret-Levrault finds himself precisely in one of the favored locations on the road network is key to his success. He was quite simply born at the right time and in the right place.

There is more, however. Minoret-Levrault is not the only member of his family involved in the expanding system of communication of the period about which we are speaking. Massin-Levrault Junior's sister is the director of the post office in Nemours, an administrative position she obtained thanks to the support of Doctor Minoret himself, who intervened with his Paris connections to get her the job: "The clerk of the justice of the peace [Massin-Levrault] . . . lived a meager existence in a house situated halfway up the Grand-Rue, of which a portion, the ground floor, was rented to his sister, director of the post office, another favor given by the doctor" (3:800). Clearly, the family has a stake in all the major axes of communication and transportation in the region. The complex interaction of the systems that transported people and letters calls for more reflection and will be the subject of a later discussion devoted to another Balzac novel, *Un Début dans la vie.* For the present, however, we should recall that the reinsertion of Doctor Minoret into life in Nemours, when he retires after a long career in Paris, is the result of an aleatory event brought about by a trip linked directly to the very network of routes controlled by Minoret-Levrault, the *maître de poste.* Doctor Minoret's rediscovery of his birthplace, the point of origin of his life and career, demonstrates in yet another form the imbrication of family networks and road networks in the novel. Here is the passage describing that rediscovery:

> [The] delightful countryside [around Nemours], that can be seen along the road from Montargis, looks like a decor from an opera because its effects are so elaborate. One morning, the doctor, who had been summoned by a rich patient in Burgundy and who was returning posthaste to Paris, having neglected to indicate at a preceding relay what road he wanted to take, was driven through Nemours unbeknownst to him. Between two naps he saw once again the countryside in which he had grown up. At that time, the doctor had just lost several old friends. . . . He was thinking of his retirement. Thus when his relay coach stopped at the top of the Grand-Rue in Nemours, he had a notion to ask about his family. (3:786)

Several elements in this passage are essential. To begin with, in the absence of the technological improvements to the road system mentioned previously, the doctor would not have been able to travel into Burgundy to treat a patient. A certain speed of travel and a certain comfort in the vehicles used for such trips are necessary before trips for medical consultations rather far outside Paris can be regularly envisaged. This passage suggests a new velocity in movement rendered possible by improved roads and carriage technology. The insistence on the doctor's haste to return to Paris calls attention to the system's potential to satisfy the desire for such speed. The branching roads on the network play a trick on the doctor, however, when the horses are changed so rapidly at one of the relay stations along the way that the driver forgets to consult with the doctor about the itinerary he prefers.[9]

By accident, through a misunderstanding about the routes to follow, Minoret finds himself once again in Nemours after many years of absence. A modern reader needs to be reminded that getting lost or taking the wrong turn was an exceedingly common occurrence in the historical period Balzac is describing. If the main roads of the national network were fairly familiar and fairly well marked, the problem of the *transversales,* the local routes that intersected with main roads, remained crucial. Intersections were not well marked, and postriders, coach drivers, and travelers were often at the mercy of a serendipitous marking system—not a system at all, actually, but a hodgepodge of local indicators. "The choice presented by the crossroad, the intersection, the bifurcation forces one to be engaged and prevents passive traveling that is inattentive to places," as Studeny writes: "There are so many ways to get lost" within the labyrinth of local bifurcations that sometimes lead to main roads and sometimes not (45–46).[10] A chance intersection provoked by a wrong turn brings the doctor once again into contact with the countryside around Nemours in the form of a dream image. He awakens in his coach from a sleep brought about by his rapid journey into Burgundy and sees a fantasy landscape, one that looks like the setting from an opera, as the text suggests, and one that suddenly appears familiar. The importance of the structure of revelation that is explicitly fashioned in this scene should not be underestimated. It calls attention directly to a stage in the transition between two types of travel. Trips on foot or by horse ambling more or less at the speed of a human walking allowed travelers to remain intimately linked to the landscape through which they were moving. At the other end of the nineteenth-century spectrum, however, were trips at the elevated speed of the train, during which the traveler was withdrawn, protected within a closed space, detached from the rushing landscape, whose appearance at high speed could only make neophytes to this kind of traveling very uneasy. The human dimensions of the voyager's experience had been surpassed by the performance of the machine.[11]

The doctor falls asleep during his return trip from Burgundy because the coach in which he is traveling transforms him and makes him a "modern" passenger. No longer a subject contemplating a landscape in the course of a trip on foot (an experience that quickly becomes lyric and is lived as a sort of communion and a knowledge imagined in a utopic mode matching the style of a traditional type of travel), the doctor has become an object enclosed in his vehicle, projected through space, and desiring only one thing—to get to where he is going as quickly as possible. Using the case of Victor Hugo, David Charles has explained how this difference between travel on foot and travel in a coach is imagined as the end of a utopia by the poet. In *Le Rhin,* Hugo waxes poetic as he describes the lyricism of traveling on foot: "On foot! One is free, joyous, belonging only to oneself. One is entirely and without interruption given over to the incidents of the road. . . . One departs, stops, starts again; bothered by nothing, held back by nothing. One goes on ahead and dreams" (Charles 20). A trip in a coach, however, as Charles demonstrates using Hugo's text, creates a very different traveler and a very different experience of movement: "Completely removed from the lyric mode, the coach passenger becomes an objet, 'shaken like a bottle that one is rinsing.' He becomes a 'machine' or that part of a machine . . . in which the quantity of movement is conserved through oscillation as it is within a closed mechanical system" (23). In its extreme form, this experience is unbearable and physically exhausting. But in a less pronounced form, when the state of the road permits it, the rocking of the coach comforts the traveler, inducing sleep and thus creating the possibility of an oneiric experience. The as-yet sketchy outlines of the process of transition between travel on foot and travel in a high-speed vehicle (a train) are visible here, and the profound psychological and physiological effects provoked by this change are already on the horizon. The doctor's detachment from the landscape surrounding him during his trip provokes an internalized self-absorption that leads toward a veritable vision of that profoundly symbolic landscape of origins, the view upon entering Nemours, his birthplace and eventually the place to which he will retire to live out the remainder of his life. What is most significant for the present argument, however, is the immediate connection made between movement along a network of roads, on the one hand, and the network of family relations, on the other. The question of genealogy with which the novel begins returns in force: "Thus when his relay coach stopped at the top of the Grand-Rue in Nemours, he had a notion to ask about his family" (3:786). The first things that come to mind when the doctor finds himself on the main street in Nemours are his own family relations. This is the intersection we must note and interpret: the network of roads and the network of collateral relations in the novel are superimposed upon one another in this moment of revelation provoked by one of the doctor's innumerable journeys.

It would be instructive to compare the description of the doctor's experience to one written by Thomas De Quincey narrating his voyages in English mail coaches. In his essay entitled *The English Mail Coach,* De Quincey chronicles his adventures as a rider of English mail coaches during his days at Oxford in the first decade of the nineteenth century (4:287–352). More particularly, in the first part of his essay, he explains how he and his classmates turned the social structure governing the passengers riding the coaches on its head. The four inside seats in the coaches had always been considered higher class than the three seats outside, on the box on the front or the back of the coach. De Quincey and his friends, however, started a craze for riding on the box. Such was the fad that they were soon pitted against the other riders on their route, who took to the idea of sitting on the box and vied with De Quincey's group for the three places on top of the coach, using bribery and ruse where necessary. Why this keen desire to sit in the most uncomfortable and inhospitable place on the coach, exposed to the elements and to the danger of being thrown from the coach in the event of an accident? De Quincey's answer to this question takes the form of a veritable phenomenology of speed on the coach roads:

> The modern modes of traveling cannot compare with the old mail-coach system in grandeur and power. They boast of more velocity, not, however, as a consciousness, but as a fact of our lifeless knowledge, resting upon *alien* evidence; as, for instance, because somebody *says* that we have gone fifty miles in the hour, though we are far from feeling it as a personal experience, or upon the evidence of a result, as that actually we find ourselves in York four hours after leaving London. Apart from such an assertion, or such a result, I myself am little aware of the pace. But, seated on the old mail-coach, we needed no evidence out of ourselves to indicate the velocity. . . . The vital experience of the glad animal sensibilities made doubts impossible on the question of our speed; we heard our speed, we saw it, we felt it as a thrilling; and this speed was not the product of blind insensate agencies, that had no sympathy to give, but was incarnated in the fiery eyeballs of the noblest amongst brutes, in his dilated nostril, spasmodic muscles, and thunder-beating hoofs. The sensibility of the horse, uttering itself in the maniac light of his eyes might be the last vibration of such a movement.[12] (302)

When Doctor Minoret travels isolated in the interior of his coach, not only is he detached from the landscape, but he is insulated from the very sensation of speed. De Quincey and his friends craved, on the contrary, the dangerous experience of the rushing landscape and wind that put the exterior voyager on the mail coach in touch with the marvelously new phenomenon of speed. When the railroad replaced the coach, the direct physical sensation of velocity, as De Quincey termed it, was forever removed from travelers, isolating them in a sort of artificial capsule that closed the passengers off from the very movement in which they were caught up. De Quincey comments: "But now, on the new system of traveling, iron tubes and boilers have disconnected man's heart from the ministers of his locomotion. . . . The galvanic cycle is broken up for ever; man's imperial nature no longer sends itself forward through the electric sensibility of the horse" (303). Whatever overwrought Romantic sensibility might be represented in such remarks, they nonetheless provide insightful witness to the sensations of speed that were connected to improved coach travel like that which conveys Doctor Minoret on his peregrinations around Paris in *Ursule Mirouët*. The coach system created the possibility of experiencing speed directly in a way that was to become impossible with the train. Sitting outside on a train at speeds in excess of forty or fifty miles an hour was untenable, even without mentioning the close tolerances with obstacles that the unvarying trajectory of the rails allowed, or, for that matter, the dense smoke produced by the firebox heating the boiler. Simultaneously, however, as Doctor Minoret's experience attests, speedy coach travel was also preparing passengers for conveyance in an enclosed space that detached the traveler from his or her own velocity.

It is important to underline that the French *malle-poste* (mail coach) system, although organized in a manner that differed considerably from its English counterpart, created related impressions of speed.[13] For the first two centuries or so of its existence, the French postal service consisted of riders carrying pouches or small trunks containing mail on routes along which relays for changing horses had been established over time by decree emanating from the king. However, beginning in 1793, specially built coaches began to be used to carry mail, in part because they were more difficult to attack and rob than lone riders (the same rationale led to the creation of English mail coaches). The following is a description of the *malle-poste:* "They looked a little like our modern paddy wagons: a large rectangular, geometrical box made out of iron, mounted very low (45 centimeters from the ground) on wheels of average diameter, with only a light box for the driver on the roof. Inside was the compartment for the mail bags and, in addition, a compartment with three seats that could be reserved by passengers, but only for long trips" (Belhoste). Sturdily built, then, and containing a considerable amount of iron, part of the structure was a mail compartment. The remaining interior space contained rudimentary seats that could be used by up to four passengers.[14] The main reason for reserving these seats exclusively for travelers going considerable distances was undoubtedly to avoid any lost time that might be incurred by negotiating with travelers if they had been picked up haphazardly at relays along the route. In other words, the passengers had to conform to the schedule of the mail, to travel with few interruptions (including during the night), and to take care of the formalities of reserving and paying for their places before the voyage commenced—in order to expedite the changing of horses at relays and to speed the mail on its way in a timely manner.

The *malle-poste* generally moved considerably faster than any other type of public coach. As Belhoste puts it: "These vehicles went very fast, pulled by four horses, burning up the road with a thunderous noise that could be heard from far away." By 1830, the average speed of the *malle-poste* over long distances was greater than that of a trot. By the middle of the century, the velocity of the gallop had been attained for extended trips—just at the moment when the *malle-poste* was beginning to be replaced by the railroad. The average speed of the service progressed slowly not because the coach and relay system failed to improve in any noticeable technological manner, but because the quality of road surfaces was so variable and problematic. As the national system of road upkeep was progressively organized and improved, especially during the July Monarchy, the new dependability of the roads allowed considerable performance gains. In any case, as Belhoste suggests, the speed of the *malle-poste* was extremely visible and noticeable to passersby, who were regularly overwhelmed by its passage, particularly by the noise generated by four horses pulling the coach along cobbled street pavement in the towns along its way. The *malle-poste* had a reputation for speed especially because it always had priority service at relays and it traveled at night. By the end of the July Monarchy, for example, *malle-poste* service between Paris and Bordeaux got travelers to their destinations in thirty-six hours, whereas the fastest trip on any private stagecoach line would have been about forty-eight hours: "It was the means of transportation for people in a hurry" (Cavaillès 227).

In *Ursule Mirouët*, then, Doctor Minoret is caught in the web of this improved road/stagecoach system, built for progressively increasing speed of circulation. He is simultaneously trapped in a network of family relations, formed in such a way as to be a system of exchange comparable to that of the road system. The logical assumption would be, in fact, that the strategic positions occupied by his cousins give them the upper hand in dealing with him and eventually in stealing his inheritance from Ursule Mirouët. Despite the striking advantage in positioning that the Minoret-Levrault-Crémière-Massin group seems to possess, however, Balzac takes pleasure in reversing the relations of force at the end of the novel and in permitting Ursule's purity and uprightness to triumph. One should remark that this very purity, as Balzac defines and characterizes it, is largely the result of her isolation from the various networks that structure the novel (genealogical and communicational). Not only is she more distant in her relation to the Minoret family than the cousins themselves (arguably not a candidate from a legal standpoint for any substantial percentage of the inheritance, as Armine Kotin Mortimer has demonstrated), but she is also presented as the one character who for a series of reasons travels very little. With the exception of her trip to Paris to help her guardian arrange for the release from debtors' prison of Savinien de Portenduère, who eventually becomes her husband, Ursule stays put, one might say. When Doctor Minoret dies and she finds herself poor and without her protector, her immediate reaction is to find another house in Nemours and to re-create the rooms in which she lived with Minoret for so many happy years before his death. In other words, she wants to re-create a home in the sense of an immovable space that is hers and that walls out any intruders. This strategy is in marked contrast with that of nearly every other important character in the novel. Those around her are constantly on the move, constantly in transit toward Fontainebleau, Paris, and more distant destinations. It is striking, for example, that Savinien must enlist as a naval officer and make a military career upon the vast spaces of the sea before he reaches the moment when he can actually claim Ursule as his wife, before he can merit her hand. The schema of immobile female and moving male is one that became a cliché in novelistic structures, as Flaubert demonstrated so categorically in *Madame Bovary,* but here it takes on a particular importance because of the strategic deployment of networking strategies that is so fundamental to *Ursule Mirouët.*

Stunningly, however, the strategic investment in all the systems of communication undertaken by the collaterals in the novel (roads, post office, family genealogies), their sordid calculations and ruses, cannot finalize their victory: "A utopic space to a certain extent," as Nicole Mozet puts it, "Balzac's Nemours is the site of a completely unexpected redefinition of filial law, conceived in terms of love and no longer in terms of blood" (219). Mortimer comes to similar conclusions when she describes the ultimate triumph of a curious mixture of spirituality and spiritism that reveals the theft perpetrated by Minoret-Levrault against his uncle and his uncle's ward, thus undoing the unbridled materialism that seems to reign without rival and permitting the restitution of at least a part of the doctor's inheritance to Ursule (860). Bernard, on the other hand, strikes a more pessimistic note in her analysis of the novel, noting that the marriage between a noble (Savinien de Portenduère) and a bourgeoise (Ursule Mirouët) at the end of the story is "unnatural" (at least according to Balzac's analysis of what is natural and therefore possible in social situations) and that it cannot therefore promise a real resolution and a lasting happiness (201). Let us not take a position here on the narrative or moral implications of this outcome chosen by Balzac (for example, on the aesthetic question of its verisimilitude or on the questions of social history raised by the choice of a utopic rather than a "realist" solution to the dilemma of inheritance created by the novel). Our remarks will be directed, rather, toward the *vehicles* that the novelist uses in order to provoke the ultimate reversal that puts the collaterals out of the picture and short-circuits all their plans. The use of term "vehicle" is motivated here by the fact that a material vehicle, a relay coach in this instance, serves as the instrument of retribution and brings about the decisive turn that allows Ursule to triumph. When the state prosecutor in Fontainebleau is informed by Mme. Minoret-Levrault, the wife of the *maître de poste* about whom we have been speaking, of the theft of Doctor Minoret's inheritance carried out by her husband, this officer of the court sends Mme. Minoret and her son Désiré immediately off to Nemours and instructs them to convince the *maître de poste* to abandon the game and give up his ill-gotten gains in order to clear the family name. The two characters jump into the first stagecoach available to take them rapidly back to Nemours to try to save Désiré's future by righting the wrong created by the theft. An accident occurs on the bridge leading into Nemours, a version of the accident imagined and anticipated by the *maître de poste,* Minoret-Levrault, in the first scene of the novel, when he was awaiting the arrival of the coach coming from Paris. Minoret-Levrault recounts the details of the accident to the court officer in Fontainebleau after the fact:

> Upon arriving at the Nemours bridge, part of the harness came loose. My wife was in the stagecoach without a servant, the horses sensed they were almost home, and my son, who feared their impatience, did not want the driver to climb down and thus got out to hook up the harness himself. At the moment when he was turning around to climb back in next to his mother, the driver lost control of the horses. Désiré was not able to jump back against the bridge parapet in time, and the running board cut his legs out from under him, whereupon he fell, and the rear wheel ran over his body. (3:984–85)

The motif of the accident implicitly traverses the entire novel in larval form only to be realized in the final pages. This death on the Nemours bridge transforms the defeat of Minoret-Levrault's plot to steal the doctor's inheritance into an accident resulting symptomatically from a traffic jam, from an interruption in the circulation of coaches on the very road network that the *maître de poste* supposedly dominates.

The accident scene must be put in parallel with the dream-like arrival of Doctor Minoret in Nemours during his rapid coach ride back toward Paris after a medical consultation, the trip that brought him back into contact with the landscape of his birth. We can now confirm even more forcefully that crucial moments in the novel are tied to intersections and incidents defined in large part by their location on the road network of which Nemours appears to be a key node. We should not forget that the accident provoking the undoing of Minoret-Levrault's plan occurs on a bridge, that most crucial passage on any road system that spans a rift, creating a path between two incompatible spatial varieties. The bridge is the figure of the strategies of intertwining at the heart of the family and road networks about which we have been reflecting. But what exactly happens on this dangerous bridge? A malfunction occurs directly related to the technological developments in the construction of coaches, which are at the heart of this unfortunate incident: one of the connecting reins breaks, the smooth functioning of the horse/coach machine is disrupted, a rift opens upon the very bridge that was supposed to join together disparate regions. A repair must be effected. Who is better placed to undertake it but Désiré Minoret-Levrault, the son of a *maître de poste*? Doubtless he spent a good part of his youth in the presence of the drivers at his father's relay station and regularly watched them repair broken parts on the coaches they drove. There would seem to be no reason to send for someone at the relay station to take care of the repair or to take the risk of having the driver climb down from his post to look after the repair himself. Désiré clearly possesses the necessary expertise. The repair is fraught with danger, however, because horses—under any circumstances—are difficult to control, always a threat to run away, eluding the mastery of the driver. This is all the more the case in the scene Minoret-Levrault recounts, since the horses are so near home and have already caught scent of the stable. They have minds of their own, as the narrator informs us. In *L'Invention de la vitesse,* Studeny reminds the reader of the banality of runaway horses in the towns and cities of the period, an experience that we moderns only rarely encounter and cannot, therefore, fathom very well: "Nothing is more banal than the runaway horse. . . . Animal furor, unpredictable, crisscrosses the daily landscape. From time to time, runaway horses send shivers through the town" (124–25). This was in part an unexpected result of the higher speeds brought about by the perfecting of the relay system and in part the result of the increase in the number of private coaches and carriages being driven in towns and cities during the period in question. Accidents and catastrophes related to these developments became a regular feature of urban landscapes: proof if one were needed that every technological development brings disadvantages along with the advantages it provides.

The accident on the Nemours bridge is a traffic jam, a symptom of the modernization of the road network that directly affects someone intimately knowledgeable about such things, Désiré, the son of the *maître de poste.* Moreover, the accident occurs in a manner that links it rather directly to the problem of family relations among the novel's collaterals, since it is occasioned by an attempt to solve the inheritance problem created by Minoret-Levrault's theft: the state prosecutor sent Mme. Minoret-Levrault and Désiré off in the coach in the first place to right the wrong done by Minoret-Levrault. The accident must be seen as a figure of the danger of the collisions between and among collaterals thrown into social circulation in the ever more rapid, ever more encumbered social mixing that characterizes Restoration society as it is described by Balzac. Collaterals clash and stagecoaches break down or crash—the story of Minoret-Levrault demonstrates starkly how these two phenomena are related. The failure of the *maître de poste* at the end of *Ursule Mirouët* would thus have a less moralizing, less ideological reading, one more linked to something that might be called the history of technologies of communication in nineteenth-century France. Balzac's perspicacity allows him to construct a novel that intricately weaves together two sets of questions that turn out to be the same: communication and genealogy.

Striking thematic and structural parallels between *Ursule Mirouët* and *La Rabouilleuse* can be discerned once the reader has understood the links between the circulation of people and information and the question of collateral relations in Balzac.[15] Once again in *La Rabouilleuse* the main narrative problem is the disposition of a substantial provincial inheritance, and, consequently, the main conflict described in the novel will pit family members and other potential heirs against one another. Briefly stated, the inheritance problem goes like this: Doctor Rouget of Issoudun sends his daughter (Agathe Rouget) to Paris to live with his wife's relatives (her brother and sister-in-law). He profits from Agathe's absence to will nearly his entire fortune to his son, Jean-Jacques Rouget. Years later, Agathe, who has lost her husband and fallen into poverty in large part because of the profligacy of her immoral eldest son, Philippe Bridau, is advised by friends to return to Issoudun in order to try to recover her rightful part of her father's inheritance from her brother. Ultimately, her dissolute son Philippe takes up the struggle personally and succeeds in wresting his mother's part from his uncle, only to slight her once again by retaining the fortune and refusing to share it either with Agathe or with his own brother Joseph.

The purpose of this brief summary of the problem created by Jean-Jacques Rouget's inheritance is to underscore the fact that once again we have a situation in which uncle and nephew are at odds, but also cousin and cousin. The question of collaterals never remains in the background for long in a Balzacian provincial novel. The uncle in *La Rabouilleuse,* Jean-Jacques Rouget, is controlled by another character, Flore Brazier, the *rabouilleuse* of the novel's title, who is in league with Maxence Gilet.[16] The two of them are after Jean-Jacques Rouget's fortune and are thus opposed to the interests of Philippe Bridau. In many ways Max is the epitome of all the complexities associated with the notion of the cousin about which we have been reflecting, because his troubled and uncertain genealogy puts him in a position that represents the essence of the bourgeois inheritance problems at stake in both *Ursule Mirouët* and *La Rabouilleuse.* Unable to claim any inheritance as a clear descendant of the Rouget family, he is nonetheless thrown in with other indirect and variously qualified potential inheritors of Jean-Jacques Rouget. He is ostensibly the son of a cavalry officer, Gilet, but his origins are exquisitely muddied in the story. His mother was a woman of questionable moral character who was romantically linked both to Lousteau and to Doctor Rouget himself. Doctor Rouget had a habit of sharing Lousteau's conquests, even though the two were staunch enemies. Max's potential triple paternity—Lousteau, Doctor Rouget, or Gilet?—is carefully maintained by Max's father, because it allows him to get support for his son (but is Max his son?) from several sources—for example, in the form of pensions to help defray the costs of Max's schooling. The complexity involved in Max's genealogical position illustrates the hidden and complex relations that conjoin cousins in the rhizomatic immixture that is at the heart of Balzac's presentation of postrevolutionary family relations.

The position Flore occupies in the inheritance structure is quite convoluted. She does not belong to the Rouget family in any strict genealogical sense, but after having first been the mistress of Doctor Rouget, she is now the object of desire of his son, Jean-Jacques, and aspires to a marriage that would make her his sole inheritor. Max and Flore manifestly function as cousins with respect to Philippe Bridau, Agathe's son, at least from a generational point of view. They are roughly the same age as Philippe, and each of them has a claim on Rouget's fortune that clashes with Philippe's own claim. This sets up a struggle among collaterals—structurally, symbolically, and even literally. To put it another way, the have-nots are only distant and relatively indirect relations of the targeted uncle, and yet Philippe, Max, and Flore, given the precarious social circumstances confronting them (none of them has any serious prospects for eventual social advancement), are destined to clash for social survival in the free-for-all of the circulation of fortunes in postrevolutionary France. The advent of a successful inheritance is the one thing that could permit them an entry into respected social circles.

These structural resemblances between the two novels quickly take on much more complex and intricate dimensions, because, as is the case in *Ursule Mirouët,* the question of genealogy and "collateral damage" is once again tied in suggestive ways to a certain strategy of speed and movement ultimately linked to displacements on roads in and around Issoudun. We can begin to explore these connections by recalling a remark made by Napoleon upon which Paul Virilio has insisted on more than one occasion: "The aptitude for war is the aptitude for movement" (*Vitesse* 31). Philippe Bridau, the great cynic and practitioner of Napoleonic tactics in Balzac's *La Rabouilleuse,* echoes this remark when he explains how he is going to outwit Maxence Gilet in order to recover his uncle's inheritance: "The talent of a general . . . consists not only in observing carefully the movements of the enemy, but also in guessing his intentions from his movements and in always modifying one's own plan to the extent that the enemy upsets it by an unexpected march" (4:493). In fact, one could easily construct an analysis of *La Rabouilleuse* around the opposition between two different types of Napoleonic veterans: Philippe Bridau, who was a cavalry officer during the Napoleonic wars, on the one hand, and Maxence Gilet, who was an infantryman, on the other. Unfortunately for Max, as we shall see, he did not follow in the military footsteps of his father, who was a cavalryman. Although the classic opposition between Paris and the provinces is the immediately apparent structuring force of the confrontation that the novel describes between these two characters, it should come as no surprise that the victory of the Parisian, Philippe Bridau, is also simultaneously the victory of the cavalry officer, of the actor in this drama whose character is summed up by his talent for moving quickly and strategically in the course of confrontations with an enemy.

Bridau's whole military career is characteristic of the type of skill he ostensibly possesses. He distinguished himself during the Napoleonic wars by his impetuosity, that is, by his readiness to throw himself at full tilt on his horse into the midst of the most violent battle. He earned his first promotion precisely in this manner: "During the French campaign, he became a lieutenant in the course of an avant-garde skirmish where his impetuosity saved his colonel" (4:296). In fact, that impetuosity is not unrelated to a certain psychological disposition that Bridau subsequently evinces for gambling. The psychological "high" that he procures at the gaming table, the sort of second state to which he seems addicted, is evidently related to the same impulsiveness that made him an effective cavalry officer during the Napoleonic campaigns. Absent the excitement of the cavalry charge, reduced to the mundane activities of civilian life in the Restoration aftermath of the Napoleonic wars, Philippe finds at the gaming table a simulation of the rapidity of the battle charge. The act of catapulting himself into enemy lines in a blind fury, the art of the cavalry officer if one may call it such, is the only thing that Philippe knows. Not surprisingly, the machine-like rapidity of the roulette wheel reproduces comparable sensations and an equal fascination. As Balzac writes at one point in the first part of the novel: "In a word, games of chance, which refused to cooperate with the rich and cold-blooded player, devoured the fortune of the player stubborn enough to let himself become dizzy with the rapid movement of this machine. The *trente-et-quarante* dealers were almost as quick as the roulette wheel" (4:333–34). It would seem that the true gambler is the one who refuses to fall prey to the vortex, to the whirlwind that is the roulette wheel or the art of dealing *trente-et-quarante* with almost sleight-of-hand skill and rapidity. Philippe is doomed at the gaming table because what he really craves is speed—not a methodical approach to rational gambling if indeed such a thing actually exists. Alternatively, it just might be the case that Philippe's experience reveals the essence of the theory of gambling that Balzac describes here and elsewhere.[17] Perhaps, in other words, gambling is invariably wedded to speed and precludes any approach that does not recognize this factor. The cold calculation of the rational gambler might be nothing but the dream of a narrator who does not even recognize the aptness of his own description of the powers of the game. Impetuosity is assuredly a regular feature of Balzac's presentation of gambling scenes.[18]

It soon becomes evident in Balzac's presentation that whenever Philippe must act quickly, whenever his aptitude for speedy tactical movement is put to the test, he has a decided advantage over the infantryman, his rival, Maxence Gilet. At a poignant moment in the novel when Max candidly evaluates his own weaknesses once he is already deep into the process leading up to his inevitable confrontation with Philippe, and when, in some sense, he sees his own death at Philippe's hands already written on the wall, he makes a very perspicacious remark that underscores what is at stake: "The course of events contains a rapidity that makes one dizzy. I took the colonel [Philippe Bridau] for one of those dashing cavalry officers who couldn't put two and two together—that was my mistake. Since I was not able to maneuver rapidly [*faire un crochet de lièvre*] in the beginning, I can only rehabilitate my good name through his death" (4:501). When things speed up, it takes someone formed by speed to make the proper tactical choices. Max's tactics, on the contrary, are constantly marked by a strategy of the stance, that is, a stable positioning in a place, the occupation and defense of a position, rather than the use of the quick maneuver that Max aptly calls a *crochet de lièvre,* literally, the hunted hare's unexpected side step, angling away from the straight line of its run. This expression is telling when one visualizes the flight of a hare, capable of turning on a dime, of veering off to the side at a very sharp angle. It is difficult, moreover, to predict the direction that such a flight will take, because its path has the form of a *randonnée,* an aleatory trajectory dictated more by unexpected obstacles than by any conscious plan. Philippe's tactics are characterized precisely by the rapid, punctual intervention of the cavalry officer, who rides down on his enemy with the chaotic rapidity of a storm and who has the maneuverability to accomplish any necessary "crochet de lièvre" along the way.

The main strategy adopted by Flore and Max in *La Rabouilleuse* is to invade and occupy Jean-Jacques Rouget's territory, to live in his house in order to spy on him and to prevent him from communicating with other people in Issoudun. Flore has already lived in the house for an extended period of time before she meets Max and falls in love with him. She graduated from being the mistress of Doctor Rouget, Jean-Jacques's father, to being Jean-Jacques's mistress. Her tenure in the house thus spans two generations. When Flore takes up with Max and Max begins to devise a strategy for getting his hands on Jean-Jacques's fortune, he conspires to persuade Flore to let him have a room in the house in order to formulate a means to control Rouget's intentions: "As soon as the officer without resources learned of the situation of Flore and Jean-Jacques Rouget, he saw more than a simple passing fancy in his liaison with the *rabouilleuse* [Flore]. To provide for his future he thus wanted all the more to become a lodger in the Rouget household" (4:404). This is a waiting game, a strategy for an infantryman content to bide his time in ambush and to wait for the proper opportunity. Jean-Jacques Rouget is already essentially isolated from the rest of the society in the town, because his relations with Flore are embarrassing to other established bourgeois residents, who have ostracized him. Max need only maintain that isolation, develop Jean-Jacques Rouget's dependence on Flore, and work toward the moment when Rouget will designate her as his sole heir.

Philippe Bridau, his enemy, implicitly recognizes the mark of the infantryman in this strategy during a conversation with his mother's lawyer, Desroches, in Paris. Desroches has succeeded in commuting Philippe's prison term for the part he played in a plot against the monarchy. The lawyer arranges for Philippe to live under house arrest in Issoudun, since Desroches has understood that only Philippe has the courage and the ruse, in short, the lack of scruples, to save his mother's inheritance. The trick was to find a legal maneuver to bring Philippe into the region where the battle for the inheritance will be engaged. When Desroches explains the situation in Issoudun to Philippe and cautions him against Max's courage, Bridau remarks, "All the better. . . . I am counting on the courage of this chap in order to succeed, because a coward would leave Issoudun" (4:469). The confidence of the infantryman has led Max to create and occupy a fortified position. By waiting calmly in ambush, however, Max has in fact committed a strategic blunder. If he had not been a courageous foot soldier, he would have fled Issoudun, doubtless with Flore and Jean-Jacques Rouget, and Philippe Bridau would therefore have had no chance to succeed in recuperating his mother's due. Philippe's evaluation of Max's behavior recognizes implicitly the type of strategy he will have to counter if he wishes to recover the inheritance. It would have been infinitely more effective for Max to have moved and moved quickly by taking to the roads and leaving Philippe trapped under house arrest in a sleepy provincial town.

The strategy of occupation devised by Max and Flore is not without its strengths, at least in the beginning. In particular, it prevents Philippe from speaking alone with his uncle at all, until ultimately Philippe decides to make this the issue of a direct confrontation. After a visit to his uncle's house during which he is invited to stay for dinner, he accepts the invitation—on the condition that Rouget take a walk with him before dinner. The conversation that ensues makes the situation explicit:

> "Oh! Don't leave yet," cried the old man [Jean-Jacques Rouget], who was encouraged by Flore's false tenderness. "Will you dine with us, Philippe?"
>
> "Yes, if you will come walk with me for an hour."
>
> "Monsieur is quite sickly," said Miss Brazier. "He did not want to go out in a carriage a minute ago," she added turning toward the old man, on whom she affixed a stare like those used to calm lunatics.

> Philippe took Flore by the arm, forced her to look at him, and looked at her just as intensely as she had just looked at her victim.
>
> "Tell me, Mademoiselle, could it be by chance that my uncle is not free to take a walk with me?"
>
> "Of course he is, Monsieur," answered Flore, who could hardly have responded otherwise.
>
> "Well, Uncle, are you coming? Please give him his cane and his hat, Mademoiselle . . ."
>
> "But usually he only goes out with me, is that not so, Monsieur?" . . .
>
> "Uncle, you will come walk with me, or I shall not come back [to your house]. . . ." (4:482)

In order to obtain a moment alone with his uncle, Philippe must force the issue and threaten to make a public scandal of Flore's influence on Rouget. The trick is to extract his uncle from the fortress and to walk with him in the street, to maneuver on the move, as it were. But if indeed Philippe gets his way in this instance, and occasionally elsewhere, it is nonetheless difficult to make inroads into the control that Flore and Max exert within the confines of the house. Philippe is forced to remain in the background, waiting for a propitious moment, preparing to move when it becomes possible. Predictably, his intervention becomes feasible only when Max and Flore venture out of the house onto the roads, that is, into the very territory that is Philippe Bridau's strategic domain. This occurs when Flore and Max need to make Rouget turn his power of attorney over to Flore. Unfortunately for their cause, they have to travel to a neighboring town to sign the appropriate legal document, because any visit to an attorney in Issoudun would be too visible and too easily countered. This projected clandestine trip must inevitably put Max and Flore at the mercy of the cavalry officer, who has judiciously deployed spies on the roads and prepared a horse to outrun the two plotters—who is, in short, ready to match any maneuver on the roads by his own quicker maneuver: "'Fario is on the lookout,' answered Philippe, 'and he is not the only one. The Spaniard found one of my former soldiers in the area, someone for whom I did a favor. Although no one suspects it, Benjamin Bourdet is under the orders of my Spaniard, who in turn put one of his horses at Benjamin's disposition'" (5:486). Every movement on the roads around Issoudun will be reported to Philippe in time for him to make the proper tactical decision. By waiting too long to move, literally to travel quickly and clandestinely on the roads around Issoudun, Max has exposed himself to an enemy whose very strength is precisely his rapid and decisive speed. This is a race on the roads that Max cannot win.

To rid himself once and for all of Maxence Gilet after he has thwarted Max's and Flore's attempt to flee Issoudun taking Jean-Jacques Rouget with them, Philippe ultimately insults him publicly and forces a duel using sabers. This is fitting, of course, because the *sabreur* (the familiar term in French for a cavalry officer, one who wields a saber), as Max once called Philippe, is thus able to use his weapon of choice, a heavy cavalry sword, better adapted to hacking at foot soldiers from astride a horse than to confronting an adversary in a dueling face-off. This is most certainly not a weapon that Max can manipulate with any expertise. To fight with a saber requires a good deal of care, because its weight makes the swordsman pay dearly for any mistake—it is simply too heavy to allow the duelist to recover from a feint that is too exaggerated or from a thrust that is too pronounced. The narrator describes the skill necessary to manipulate this weapon:

> Victory depends on a false movement, an error of calculation, lightning quick, to which one must react instinctively. For a period of time, as short for the onlookers as it seems long for the adversaries, the struggle consists in observing, an activity in which the forces of the soul and the body are absorbed, all of this disguised by feints, whose slowness and apparent prudence seem to suggest that neither of the antagonists wishes to fight. This moment, followed by a rapid and decisive struggle, is horribly intense for a connoisseur. (4:509)

Here is a fight that can be won only by impetuosity applied at the right moment, when one must profit from an improper feint by the adversary in order to thrust forward with a maximum of energy and a minimum of hesitation. Small wonder that Philippe dispatches Maxence Gilet into the next world in very little time and with maximum efficiency.

"People like that move quickly," says Desroches, while describing the legal maneuvers in which Philippe Bridau engages once he has rid himself of Max (4:516). Or, as Bixiou puts it so aptly later in the novel, Philippe is a *Méphistophélès à cheval,* "a Mephistopheles on horseback" (4:535). Philippe must move to make certain that his uncle's inheritance does not escape him and revert back to his mother and his brother. We shall not follow the rest of the details of his maneuvers and instead shall turn our attention to the rather extraordinary conclusion that Balzac gives to *La Rabouilleuse,* extraordinary on two counts in relation to the arguments made here about the novel. The first count, the more explicit one, has to do with Philippe's death. Having lost in a stock market speculation a large part of the fortune that he was able to muster using his uncle's inheritance, Philippe decides to reenlist in the cavalry. Sent to Algeria for the beginnings of the colonial wars, he languishes in his post as a colonel with little hope for advancement, because he has lost the support of crucial superiors in Paris. His exaggerated cruelty causes him to lose the respect of his men as well, and the result is fatal. In the course of an encounter with a group of Muslim soldiers, he throws himself into their midst, exactly as he did when he earned his lieutenant's commission years earlier. Abandoned by his men, however, he is hacked to death in the most violent manner:

> During a retreat when the French forces were outnumbered by the Arabs, he suddenly turned and went on the offensive, throwing himself against the enemy followed only by a company of soldiers. They encountered a large number of Arabs. The combat was bloody, atrocious. . . . Seeing that their colonel was surrounded, the soldiers who were distant from the fray judged that it was not worthwhile to perish uselessly while trying to free him. . . . Philippe suffered a horrible death, because his head was cut off after he fell, hacked almost to pieces by the enemies' yataghans. (5:540)

Live impetuously, die impetuously, Balzac tells us explicitly.

The second fascinating twist that marks the end of the novel has to do with the manner in which Philippe loses his ill-gotten fortune. This happens in the course of a stock market speculation. More will be said about the characteristics of stock speculation and its relation to the notion of speed in the exchange of information when we analyze Stendhal's *Lucien Leuwen,* but the conclusion of *La Rabouilleuse* already contains some of the elements to which we shall return. Once he has recovered his uncle's inheritance, Philippe fails in an attempt to arrange a marriage with a noble family, largely because his friends are angry at him for his totally absorbing self-interest that prevents him from maintaining truly reciprocal relations with them. He reflects on what might be necessary in order to win the hand of the daughter of the marquis de Langeais. Ten million francs, suggests Rastignac immediately and ironically (the sum is large and indicates explicitly the social distance between Philippe and Mlle. de Langeais). Philippe instantly takes this suggestion seriously and indicates not only that he already has three million but that he is ready and able to speculate in the stock market in order to make the rest in short order. This casual and ambitious remark draws the attention and the secret ire of both Nucingen and du Tillet, bankers who are sitting at the table with Philippe, and they tacitly agree—one glance exchanged between Nucingen and du Tillet suffices—to get their hands on Philippe's money by manipulating him in the stock market: "Indeed, these two members of the most exclusive banking community were placed at the heart of political life in a way that allowed them to play the stock market almost with certainty against Philippe, given the necessary time. Even if all the probabilities would appear to be in his favor, those probabilities would really be tilted their way" (4:539).[19] If properly timed, a rise or a fall of the market can wipe out an entire fortune overnight, as speculators have known from the beginning of the existence of the market. Eventually, Philippe wagers nearly his whole fortune on a market rise in July 1830, while Nucingen and du Tillet, anticipating the revolution of 1830, adopt a bear strategy.[20] They win, Philippe loses—end of story. Just as rapidly as he threw his money on the roulette table in the old days of his drinking binges, he enters into the market fray with no hesitation, without reflection. In the blink of an eye, the battle is over.

Balzac remains in character with his description of Philippe Bridau here and brings his story to a dual conclusion in a manner that clearly highlights the lesson of speed that is at the heart of the novel. The logic of the struggle among collaterals that resulted in a victory by the one cousin, Philippe Bridau, who was distinguished by the quickness of his maneuvering—on the roads, but also generally in a whole series of his other tactical choices—is carried here to a logical conclusion that strangely resembles the traffic jam and the accident at the end of *Ursule Mirouët*. Certainly Philippe's death in the mêlée of the battlefield is the direct result of his maneuvering into a position where he can no longer call upon his characteristic speed of movement. Surrounded, he is doomed. But his failed stock market speculation may also be viewed as a catastrophe not unlike what happens, for example, with the increased speeds of vehicles on roads and later on the railroad. There are speed limits beyond which one loses control. The quickness of market fluctuations, fueled by telegraph messages as we shall soon see, can have accidental results that are infinitely more devastating than what occurs when information transits more slowly.

2 *Intersections: Relays, Stagecoaches, Walks (Balzac* bis*)*

So fascinated was Balzac by the question of roads and transportation that within a year after composing *Ursule Mirouët,* he returned to the subject of road travel in *Un Début dans la vie.*[1] This short novel opens with an extended sequence set in and around a coach on the road between Paris and L'Isle-Adam in the Oise Valley. If *Ursule Mirouët* tells the story of a *maître de poste,* one of the managers of the new road system that was being put into place and improved at the end of the eighteenth and beginning of the nineteenth centuries, *Un Début dans la vie* turns the perspective around and puts the reader into a coach itself at the level of the driver and his passengers. Curiously enough, the first sentence of the novel refers to the rise of the railroad: "In a not too distant future, the railroad will make certain economic activities disappear and will modify others—especially those involved with the different means of transportation available in the Paris region" (1:731). As the Pléiade editor of the novel, Pierre Barbéris, remarks, however, not a single Balzac character ever travels by train in *La Comédie humaine.* In *Un Début dans la vie,* the coming of the railroad functions as the backdrop for an extended discussion about the reorganization of coach services in and around Paris in the early 1820s. If the railroad is occasionally mentioned in *La Comédie humaine*—and specifically in *Un Début dans la vie* only as a possibility still well over the historical horizon—this is because the time frame of Balzac's historical description of the Restoration precedes the rapid development of the rail network that began to gather momentum only in the 1840s in France. As Barbéris suggests, the rarity of remarks about the railroad system in Balzac's texts—only a handful in the whole *Comédie humaine*—is an indication of how slowly the railroad penetrated into crucial domains of French economic and social life during the Restoration and the July Monarchy. It is not surprising, then, that Balzac was more interested in the interstices of the road transportation network as its players were forced to adapt to the concentration of capital and thus to the rise of larger firms that were consolidating routes and increasingly becoming entities with which to reckon.

Balzac's description of the *voiture de Pierrotin,* the small local line that is exploited by the novelistic character Pierrotin between L'Isle-Adam and Paris in *Un Début dans la vie,* contains considerable detail and allows us to learn significantly more about the elements that structure the transportation system of the Restoration. In *Ursule Mirouët* a certain exactness in coach scheduling resulting from improvements in the road network and in technologies of coach construction was clearly visible. This programmed precision is explicitly suggested by the worried behavior of Minoret-Levrault, the *maître de poste* in Nemours, who anxiously awaits in the novel's first scene the arrival of a coach coming from Paris, delayed for unknown reasons. Balzac's description of coach scheduling at the beginning of *Un Début dans la vie* provides more depth and complexity, further developing the allusive indications provided in *Ursule Mirouët.* In the first place, Balzac speaks of what he calls a certain "elasticity" in the routine of the runs that Pierrotin's coach makes between the capital and the provincial town. The departure from Paris toward L'Isle-Adam is supposedly set for four o'clock in the afternoon on weekdays and the return trip from L'Isle-Adam for eight o'clock in the morning, but "in the evening, the departure scheduled for four was regularly delayed until four-thirty, and the one scheduled in the morning, although it was announced for eight o'clock, never took place before nine" (1:737).

Things have not yet reached the point of exactness and precision that became the standard for railroad command and control systems toward the middle of the century. The railroad called for a time calculated in minutes and seconds if disaster was to be avoided.[2] The recurring delay is not systematic; it varies to fit the season:

> This system was, moreover, quite elastic. In summer, the golden season for transport companies, the rules for departures, rigorous for strangers, were bent only for natives of the region. This method gave Pierrotin the possibility of pocketing the price of a ticket twice, when a passenger who lived in the region came early and asked for a seat that had already been sold to a *one-time passenger* [*oiseau de passage,* Balzac's italics], who,

> unhappily, was late. This elasticity might not be viewed very favorably by moral purists, but Pierrotin and his colleague justified it by the *harsh times,* by their losses during the winter season, by the pressing necessity to buy better coaches, and finally by the strict observance of the rules printed on the schedules, copies of which were exceedingly rare and given only to occasional travelers stubborn enough to demand them. (1:737)

This explanation of Pierrotin's methods reminds the reader that despite improvements that had benefited the road system by the early 1820s, winter (mid-autumn through mid-spring, in fact) was nonetheless a very difficult season during which service was often disrupted because of the deterioration of road surfaces caused by rain, freezes, and snow.[3]

More important in the passage, however, is the description of the strategies employed by Pierrotin to deal with the rules and the laws governing his activities. Room remains for maneuvering in the space of play left within any domain defined by a set of rules, and it becomes evident, as one follows Balzac's analysis a little further, that this space of play is precisely what allows the coach transportation system to function. Absent a certain amount of tolerance toward restrictions, the system would seize up and become unworkable. Balzac indicates elsewhere, for example, that in addition to fiddling with departure times in order to sell some seats twice, Pierrotin is an expert at running little errands for his customers, delivering small packages, messages, and occasional letters (activities for which the post office supposedly had the monopoly). He thus commands a continued loyalty from the travelers in the region he serves, who know they can count on him for much more than simple transportation to and from Paris. He is, moreover, an expert at eluding the system of *passe-debout,* that is, the official permission necessary to avoid paying taxes on goods brought into protected customs regions. In addition, during seasons when travel demand is heavy, Pierrotin regularly overloads his coach by carrying more passengers than is permitted, a practice that becomes under certain circumstances a little too evident to the authorities despite his good relations with them. Before Pierrotin's coach enters towns that have police posts, the supplementary travelers are obliged to get out and walk, later regaining their places in the coach when it leaves town—out of sight of the authorities. Finally, Pierrotin has a second coach, or, rather, a carriage of sorts, a hybrid vehicle like many still plying the roads in provincial France during this period, which he uses during the good seasons and on which he does not pay the proper taxes: "This might seem extraordinary today, but at the beginning, the tax on vehicles, implemented with a sort of timidity, allowed transporters to engage in these kinds of petty fraud; they were rather happy to *thumb their noses* [*faire la queue*] at the tax inspectors, as they put it. . . . Everything has its age of innocence, even the tax authorities" (1:740). The early period of a progressive regulatory process always appears after the fact to be a happy time before all the loopholes were closed. In short, Pierrotin protects his economic niche very well in an increasingly monopolized environment.[4]

It is instructive from this perspective to reflect on the differences between Minoret-Levrault (in *Ursule Mirouët*) and Pierrotin. Minoret-Levrault has a wide overview of the network and controls key nodes. Pierrotin works in its interstices and finds its weak points where he can escape the gaze of the *maître de poste,* who is allied with the larger monopolists and with the authorities—and whose goal would more likely be to rationalize the system and to render transparent the parts he wishes to control rather than to maintain the loopholes from which Pierrotin profits. Of course, at their own level, the *maîtres de poste* had other loopholes to manipulate.

With *Un Début dans la vie,* then, we encounter again the question of schedules and timetables. More needs to be said about this before we continue an analysis of the novel's opening sequence, in order to establish a wider context for the problem of time and travel that Balzac treats both in *Ursule Mirouët* and in *Un Début dans la vie.* Our reading of *Ursule Mirouët* made the claim that a certain expectation concerning chronological exactness was detectable in the structure of the first scene, and this led to the suggestion that Balzac was expressing in his manner a sociological development in time management and in expectations about speed that occurred before the railroad. What contributes to this phenomenon? How is it that the public comes to expect regularity and exactness when it comes to overland travel? These are vast questions, evidently, that can be addressed only partially here. In his short essay presenting the correspondence of administrators of the British mail coach system during the last decade of the eighteenth century, Edmund Vale quotes from Thomas De Quincey's *The English Mail Coach,* to which we referred earlier. Says De Quincey: "These mail-coaches, as organized by Mr. Palmer, are entitled to circumstantial note from myself, having had so large a share in the anarchies of my subsequent dreams; an agency which they accomplished, first, through velocity, at that time unprecedented . . . [and] through the conscious presence of a central intellect, that, in the midst of vast distances—of storms, of darkness, of danger—overruled all obstacles into one steady co-operation to a national result."[5] Vale goes on to quote a footnote conjoined to this passage in De Quincey's essay: "One case was familiar to mail-coach travelers, where two mails in opposite directions, north and south, starting at the same minute from points six hundred miles apart, met almost constantly at a particular bridge which bisected the total distance" (1 [4:289 in De Quincey]). Two crucial issues are at stake in these remarks. First, the mail coach system, after it was reorganized and streamlined in the last decade of the eighteenth century in England, impressed those who frequented it by a speed of travel unknown before that time. Second, the development of that speed went hand in hand with an organizational push toward chronological precision creating unprecedented regularity, such that coaches beginning from different locations and traveling rapidly could nonetheless routinely meet at the same place.

Edmund Vale chronicles the bureaucratic battles fought by a series of outstanding administrators, John Palmer in particular, who were able to transform the English mail system within the space of a decade. These reforms required a combination of better roads, redesigned coaches, and uniform administrative procedures and responsibilities. In a word, the developments were not unrelated to what Turgot had undertaken in 1775 for the general coach transportation system in France.[6] They culminated in the introduction of precise timing in the routing of the mail coaches leaving London, as well as those arriving there from outlying localities. There was a limit to the efficiency possible in distributing mail if the coaches carrying it out of London toward the countryside and vice versa did not meet other coaches servicing local routes at precise times. Too much time was lost if the mail had to wait at such points of intersection.[7] The solution was to establish timetables, but the difficulty in doing so was immediately apparent. The technological means and the international coordination necessary for the later system of Greenwich Mean Time, the international synchronization of time, simply did not exist during the historical period in question. Such a thing would remain impossible until the installation of an extensive electrical telegraph network that would allow the broadcast of a base time almost instantaneously across wide geographical reaches. The infrastructure and political climate allowing an international agreement establishing Greenwich Mean Time would not be in place until 1883.

In the late eighteenth century, time was synchronized in each town by a local sundial, and thus regions to the west of London ran behind London time, while regions to the east ran ahead of London time. John Palmer, the administrator of the British General Post Office who was most responsible for the installation of the mail coach system, was undeterred by this logistical problem and invented an ingenious solution. The General Post Office guard on each individual mail coach would carry a timepiece that "could be easily regulated to gain or lose as required during the given time of a long journey. . . . On long journeys it had to be handed in to the postmaster at certain points to be checked or exchanged for another. At these places the postmasters had keys to unlock the case to wind or regulate the time-piece. At every check-point the instrument had to be signed for and its number entered on the time-bill" (Vale 47–48). This signaled the end of the freedom that the mail coaches had enjoyed to run loosely on their own time and speeded up operations considerably. It led, as could be imagined, to labor resistance on the part of the post office guards, who did not take easily to the disciplining of their performance that such a system allowed. The new time constraints radiated outward to all the other personnel connected to the coach system, down to the lowly stable boys at the relay points, for example, who now had to answer to a post office guard increasingly in a hurry to get the horses changed and to continue on his route to avoid jeopardizing his job. Of course, travelers using mail coaches also had to conform to a new standard. The ubiquitous nature of the General Post Office suggests that the reforms leading to such a precision exchange system for mail must certainly have played an important role in establishing norms of punctuality and speed that had not existed in England before (the reader should recall that the first section of De Quincey's *The English Mail Coach* is entitled "The Glory of Motion," which captures some of the exhilaration travelers in the mail coaches must have felt).

The fiscal difficulties of the end of the *ancien régime* and the disorder of the revolutionary period in France created multileveled blockages in the pursuit of the reforms Turgot had begun to institute in France starting in 1775, and which had brought about his own downfall as minister within a year after he announced the reforms. It could be argued, however, that the period of the First Empire put the question of velocity and precision in road travel and mail circulation back at the center of French national concerns. Not only did Napoleon reestablish a firm central administration to oversee the road transportation of mail and passengers—with a method of accountability that went directly up the ranks to his own person—but he understood as a military strategist the importance of a road system that would allow rapid deployment of his troops to all corners of Europe: "In his mind, the strategic and political point of view was predominant. Roads had to carry to the farthest regions the power of his administration and his armies" (Petot 405). It was not enough just to arrive at the desired destination; one had to be able to get there quickly: "The Emperor demanded excellent and rapid service. The watchword during his entire reign was speed" (Cavaillès 216). The necessity for rapid exchanges of strategic messages and for rapid movement of troops led the emperor to take an interest in the French road system that had not been duplicated by any ruler or administrator since Turgot. His legendary attention to detail had him intervening down to the level of localized decision making, when he often decided, for example, where new roads were to pass, how the bridges necessary for new routes were to be constructed, how to apply and benefit from cost-saving construction techniques, and the like.

Within the mail system, Napoleon reestablished the *estafette* method of sending important documents. Although it had been used in the seventeenth century, it had fallen out of favor and had to be reactivated by the imperial regime. The revamping of this service is one of the important elements that caused the questions of time and speed to intersect symptomatically under the First Empire, as they did with the mail coach system in England in the 1790s. The following is Eugène Vaillé's succinct description of the *estafette* system: "The system consisted in giving each *maître de poste* over a given route the responsibility to send express letters with one of his postriders to the next relay station. These letters were locked in a bag for which the sender and the receiver—frequently the emperor himself and the general director of the Post Office—each had a key. The packet was accompanied by a notebook where the times of departure and arrival at each relay were inscribed all the way to the destination point" (*Histoire des postes* 38). This means of sending documents mobilized extra personnel in the relays along the way and allowed Napoleon and the director of his postal system, Lavalette, to know with dramatically increased precision where a given document had been or was going to be at a specific time. They were thus able to keep a very close watch on the operation of the relays and to focus their criticism on places that did not perform up to par. As Lavalette wrote in his memoirs: "I was able to know that there was a day's delay on a trip of 1,000 miles. . . . The emperor received in eight days responses to letters sent to Milan and in fifteen days those to Naples" (quoted in Cavaillès 216).

The time pressures that were applied with this increased surveillance also augmented the responsibilities and limitations placed on the *maîtres de poste.* The legislation of the period called upon them to stay at their relay stations at all times, to give six months' notice of their decision to give up their relays, to be responsible for any accidents caused by horses that were not suitable for service, and to hire postriders who had worked elsewhere in the system only if they had certificates of good behavior (Cavaillès 217). One can easily see parallels with the new modes of performance required of the English mail coach guards in the evolution of the English General Post Office during the 1790s. No longer were the post relay owners able to set all of the parameters of their time responsibilities. These new practices instituted in France during the empire undoubtedly had an effect on how those connected with the service understood and lived speed, distance, and time. Without question that effect radiated out to wider cultural practices—witness Minoret-Levrault's behavior at the beginning of *Ursule Mirouët.*

One can, in fact, make a broader argument about these new transportation techniques. Such an argument has been proposed by Richard John, a historian who has recently written on the development of the U.S. Postal Service between the end of the eighteenth century and the middle of the nineteenth. John asserts, and the evidence for this assertion is quite convincing, that a new and efficient communication network was created in the United States before the railroad and thus in the absence of any of the technological advances to which historians always point when describing communication structures in the nineteenth century, specifically, the railroad and the electrical telegraph: "To an extent perhaps hard to imagine today, it was neither the railroad nor the telegraph nor even the commercialization of fossil fuel, but rather the stagecoach and the postrider that liberated Americans from their crippling dependence on the vagaries of geography, wind, and water" (110). Although clear differences exist between the transformation and reforms accomplished in the American postal system of the early nineteenth century and those characteristic of England, France, and the German states, the argument nonetheless holds *mutatis mutandis* for European countries and states as well. It is true, for example, that the postal reforms in the United States in the first part of the nineteenth century amounted to a government subsidy program for the development of regular stagecoach service to all parts of the new republic, thinly populated or not. Subcontracting of mail delivery was a means for providing fledgling stagecoach lines with a stable financial basis upon which to build and thus to provide service to regions where very few people lived. This kind of synergy between postal delivery and stagecoach lines, between the circulation of messages and the transportation of people, did not exist in anything like the same terms in France. The French equivalent of the beginning of reform and thus of a certain government subsidy in the development of the stagecoach system would be Turgot's measures of 1775, evidently quite different in form from what occurred in America. A second moment of government subsidy occurred in France in 1805 when a law was promulgated obliging private stagecoach companies to pay a tax to the *maîtres de poste* on established post roads if they did not use the horses provided by the *maîtres de poste.* This had the effect of reinforcing the national system of post relays and of rendering their service more uniform (Cavaillès 220). In any case, as far as the mail system was concerned, the British and the French long saw postal delivery as an important source of state revenue, while the American postal system was viewed by the American federal government as an administration that should reinvest any revenues produced into improving the postal network itself, instead of filling federal coffers with revenue to be disbursed in other ways. Thus postal charges remained relatively high in England and France long after they had fallen to low levels in the United States.

Despite these considerable differences, however, John's argument concerning the fundamental principles of the reorganization of communicational networks in the developing Western countries retains broad validity. The continued development of stagecoach service and its gradual coordination with mail delivery coaches (themselves transporting passengers) required the progressive institutionalization of much more regular scheduling practices. In turn, these developments, taken together with road improvements and improvements in the construction of stagecoaches, contributed greatly to producing considerable gains in speed and thus considerable time savings for both travelers and postal communication well before the development of railroad technologies, which themselves thus benefited from a whole host of organizational practices that had already become well ingrained in the culture of the first half of the nineteenth century. Using technologies that differed very little from those of much older cultures (the wheel and animal energy), early-nineteenth-century European and American societies created a communicational system that represented a quantum leap in improvement compared to what had existed prior to the period.

Not only does *Un Début dans la vie* bring Balzac's reader back to questions of time and velocity associated with travel by coach or stagecoach, it opens up additional dimensions for an analysis of such communication in the first half of the nineteenth century. Recall that in *Ursule Mirouët* Doctor Minoret traveled apparently alone in a *chaise de poste,* that is, a small, rather rudimentary carriage that he doubtless rented from one of the *maîtres de poste* along the route he took. There is no mention of mail or of mail coaches in the scene described in *Ursule Mirouët.* At stake in our analysis of the travel scene in *Ursule Mirouët* was the doctor's inner state brought about by the conditions accompanying his physical movement in space. In *Un Début dans la vie,* we encounter a situation characterized not by a solitary traveler in a small carriage but by multiple passengers in a larger conveyance. Moreover, if indeed Pierrotin's coach is by no means a mail coach, questions of messages and communication are nonetheless at the heart of the first part of the story. There may not be mail in the coach in the formal sense of the term, but Balzac explicitly makes the transporting of documents a fundamental element of his description: the moving of people and the moving of messages intersect in the novel in a manner that must be explored.

In his *Relays: Literature as an Epoch of the Postal System,* Bernhard Siegert describes how the transportation of people and of messages in the form of letters was structurally equivalent during much of the first half of the nineteenth century in Europe.[8] Specifically, postage rates mimicked the cost of conveying passengers, because the rate for a letter depended not on its weight/volume alone but principally on the geographical distance the letter was going to travel, just as was the case for voyagers traveling to destinations. Moreover, a significant percentage of passengers transported were conveyed in mail coaches or, if not in mail coaches, at least along postal routes using the same relays and horses as those used by mail carriers:

> From the seventeenth century until the mid-nineteenth, postage for the transportation of symbols was economically assessed according to geography in the same way as the transportation of bodies for the simple reason that both were accomplished by the same means of transportation. The same postal carriage could convey both a letter and its writer. The subject of the letter's text (Todorov's *sujet d'énoncé*) and the subject of the letter's speech act (Todorov's *sujet d'énonciation*) fell under the jurisdiction of one and the same institution of exchange. The postage for a letter thus had to represent the amount of distance to be covered and the weight of the letter as precisely as possible, as if handling the letter involved the actual person. Consequently, symbols could hold forth as a replacement for bodies; letters could be imagined as the proxies of an absent body. (15–16)

Siegert calls attention to this situation in order to argue that the theory of literary representation most symptomatically embodied by Goethe in the German tradition is a function of a certain technology of communication that existed at the end of the eighteenth century and the beginning of the nineteenth. In Siegert's view, then, literary representation is not an unchanging, ideal structure but is instead a technologically dependent constellation that is transformed as historical conditions evolve. If historical change is slow, a representational system can appear very stable, in fact, it can appear to be eternal. In moments when the rhythm of technological change becomes rapid—as has been the case since the second half of the nineteenth century—the conditions of language use and representation become more visible, since their interaction with quickly evolving technologies of communication destabilizes them and shows their dependence on such technologies.

Siegert's argument owes much to Friedrich Kittler's work on what Kittler has called discourse networks.[9] The *mise-en-parallèle* of the transportation of people and messages is extremely suggestive. During the first half of the nineteenth century, the writer of the letter and the subject matter of the letter itself (as inscribed on a sheet of paper) were conveyed by the same vehicle under equivalent conditions of passage: both occupied parts of the same space (the carriage in which they traveled) and the economic terms of their conveyance were similar (both were charged based essentially on distance traveled). This structure gives to the signs contained in the letter a status that is indubitably bound up with the materiality of travel conditions to which they are tributaries. If indeed Goethe considered the texts he produced and, in particular, the letters he wrote, to be a veritable physical extension of his mental being, a presence in his absence, as Siegert claims, the logic of Goethe's conception of representation is not the result simply of a literary theory posited as an ideal: it is also driven by the technologies of transportation that were characteristic of his age. Since Goethe and his letters transited overland by the same methods, he could more easily see them as pure extensions of himself.

Without reproducing all of the terms of Siegert's argument, *Un Début dans la vie* nonetheless creates a highly interesting variation on the theme of the absence/presence of an author with respect to the written word that ostensibly represents him and that is conveyed between two geographical points along a land route. Both an "author" and certain documents representing him are, in fact, in transit in the same conveyance, Pierrotin's coach, in the first part of Balzac's story. As the novel opens, Pierrotin is preparing for his four o'clock departure from Paris for L'Isle-Adam, and the passengers are arriving to take their places in the coach. The chance intersection of the six passengers in the coach, soon complicated by the common interests that subtly link them to each other, reproduces a literary theme that can be found in other narratives of the period. The random meeting of travelers in the same coach, who proceed to strike up a conversation during the trip, is an inevitable leitmotiv of a period when the frequency of coach travel was increasing dramatically. When one adds to that formula an additional complexity, namely, the intersection of life stories related to one another (relations of which the travelers in the coach have no inkling as the journey begins), the elements of an interesting period novel have been assembled. Balzac used the formula in the earliest novel that found its way into *La Comédie humaine, Les Chouans,* about which more later, when he brought Marie de Verneuil and the marquis de Montauran together in a coach on the road to Fougères.

Most interesting in *Un Début dans la vie* is the way the trip causes the intersection of the physical body of its key passenger, the comte de Sérisy, with a document that represents him—a sales contract that the count wants signed by the seller in order to add a piece of land (a farm called Les Moulineaux) to his country estate (Presles). The person of the count and this legal text transit along the same route and in the same conveyance, but the coincidence of their presence one with the other is at first hidden from the travelers in the coach, including the count himself. When Georges Marest, a clerk in the office of Sérisy's notary, climbs into Pierrotin's coach to begin the journey to L'Isle-Adam, he places a document carrier under the cushion of his seat: "Georges . . . got into the coach, with a condescending air, throwing a large satchel [*portefeuille*] onto the seat, which he then put under the cushion" (1:770). The *portefeuille* is symbolically none other than the *malle* of the postal service, a satchel containing documents to be transported during this trip. The count, the other part of this equation of person and document, has opted to travel incognito in the coach in order to arrive unannounced at his country estate. Georges does not know the count as the voyage begins, because he has never met Sérisy, nor does the count know that Georges is a messenger for Crottat, his personal notary. In the satchel Georges is carrying with him is an *acte de vente,* a sales contract drawn up by Sérisy's lawyer at the count's behest. The document outlines the terms of a legal act, the purchase of Les Moulineaux, as indicated above. It is unusual for someone of Sérisy's social stature to be involved personally in such a transaction. It is, moreover, quite singular for him to travel in a public coach, on a trip for which under normal circumstances he would use his own carriage. Ordinarily the count would not have to be present for the sale of a piece of property. A simple signature would do, the legal document could stand in his stead, and the whole transaction could well be completed by any one of Sérisy's legal representatives.

In this instance, however, the notary Crottat and the count's lawyer, Derville, have counseled Sérisy to go in person to try to close the deal over dinner with the owner of Les Moulineaux, Margueron. Crottat and Derville, very familiar with the ruses of apparently thick-headed provincials, adept at tricking supposedly more sophisticated Parisians, fear that the sale is in jeopardy. Unless the count can pull off the deal in a lightning *coup* over dinner with Margueron in the course of a surprise visit to the country, Derville despairs of ever completing the purchase. The count and the document that is to cement his hold on Les Moulineaux and that simultaneously empowers his representatives to act on his behalf—to stand in for him, to *be* him in this instance—thus find themselves together in the same coach.

The count is the first of the passengers to realize that he is traveling in the presence of the very text that represents him. By the time the coach stops at the first relay station in Saint-Denis, Sérisy, intrigued by Georges's manner and his garrulous nature during the first part of the trip, has begun to wonder if indeed Georges might be Crottat's clerk and therefore the messenger conveying the *acte de vente* to be used in negotiating for the purchase of the farm. Sérisy briefly stretches his legs, but he returns to the coach while the other travelers are taking refreshments inside the inn, whereupon he looks in the *portefeuille* Georges has stored under his cushion to see what it contains:

> Intrigued by the mixture of apparent truths and jokes in Georges's conversation, the count quickly stepped into the coach, looked under the cushion at the satchel placed there by this enigmatic character, where Pierrotin had informed him he could find it, and read the letters engraved in gold: "Crottat, notary." Immediately, the count took the liberty of opening the satchel, fearing rightly that Papa Léger might be seized by a similar curiosity. He removed the document concerning the Moulineaux farm, folded it, put it in the pocket of his coat, and returned to examine the other travelers. (1:781)

Two remarks are immediately pertinent to explain more fully what happens in this scene. First, Pierrotin, who knows the count, has been won over to the count's cause with the promise of a liberal tip if he does not reveal the count's identity during the trip. Thus Pierrotin is on the count's side and has already answered queries about Georges by volunteering information about the existence of the satchel in question. Second, when one of the passengers, Léger, first gives his name as the trip begins in Paris, Sérisy immediately recognizes him as the rival would-be buyer of Les Moulineaux, the very person against whom Sérisy is struggling in order to purchase the farm. Recognizing Léger and recognizing as well that he is a wily provincial fully capable of gaining whatever advantage possible by doing something like what the count himself does—by looking in the clerk's satchel—Sérisy has to act preemptively, because he must find out what is in the satchel before Léger. Thus Sérisy discovers a written text, his own (the *acte de vente*), in the very coach in which he is riding. He promptly seizes it, reunites it with its owner (himself), thus re-creating a coincidence between author and text. His haste to accomplish this act demonstrates ultimately that one was not the other: the sales contract, the written text at stake here, may have represented Sérisy, but it was not Sérisy, and Sérisy opts to remove it from circulation in order to eliminate the complexity created by its existence, that is, the fact that any third party might intercept it and turn it to other purposes. The sales contract has a certain independent status that the count chooses to terminate.

The written text is not simply an extension of Sérisy's self, as Balzac's story makes very clear. It has a life of its own; it is subject to discovery by an interested third party, who could then use the information it contains against its author, in ways that its author cannot control. Letters do not always arrive at their destinations, and the vagaries of their wanderings reveal the limits of the notion of identity in the structure of representation, as Jacques Derrida has shown us with a great deal of subtlety and irony in *La Carte postale.* If a letter were always read only by its addressee, things would be different and considerably simpler. Once it is thrown into circulation, however, all sorts of third parties have access to it (legally or illegally). It is no longer a seamless expression of its author's intentions, no longer simply an extension of the identity of its author. Instead it possesses an existence and potential effects independent of what its author may have intended.

Siegert, an astute reader of Derrida, argues from similar premises. When concluding that the postal rate system reproduced an ideology of identity between writer and letter, precisely because it treated passengers and letters in the same way, he simultaneously underlines the fact that this logic is circular. In other words, the rate system about which Siegert speaks both reflects an ideology of textual production that posits an identity between authors and their texts and materially contributes to the reinforcement and "naturalization" of such an ideology: letter and passenger are assessed rates based on distance traveled in a similar manner and both travel in the same conveyances because, *and therefore* (as the ideological reasoning would have it), they are equivalent. But despite this ideological nexus, Balzac's *Un Début dans la vie* demonstrates strikingly that once thrown into the transportation network, the letter and its author are subject to separation, to a rift that undermines their identity and interchangeability and ultimately threatens unforeseen consequences. In the case of Sérisy, exposure of the *acte de vente* to a perspicacious and dangerous third party (Léger) in Pierrotin's coach before the right moment will abort the property purchase, which is the object of Sérisy's trip to the country.

It is easy to argue in a resolutely materialist way, however, without any recourse to Derrida's critique of metaphysics, that letters have never gotten to their destinations in any straightforward manner and that this has been the case ever since the beginnings of the modern postal system in Europe during the Renaissance. The same historian who wrote a history of the French postal system also wrote a history of the infamous *Cabinet noir*, the secret service created by the French monarchy during the *ancien régime* to open the letters of anyone, from foreign diplomats to private citizens, in order to discover useful secrets.[10] As Voltaire is reputed to have said, no minister "who was in charge of the Post Office ever opened the letters of any private citizen, except when he needed to know what they contained" (quoted in Vaillé, *Cabinet* 3). The point of Voltaire's extremely ironic comment is that the government constantly opened letters sent by all sorts of citizens for all sorts of reasons—and this practice continued well into the nineteenth century.[11] The principle of private communication via the postal system was established only slowly in Western Europe and later the United States. Seen from a certain perspective, the rise of the well-known nineteenth-century figure of the private detective is intimately linked to the debate about the privacy of postal correspondence. In the United States, special agents, "invisible" agents, as they were sometimes called, were already being used by the postal service to investigate breaches in the security of the post office by the early 1830s.[12] In an utterly fascinating way in Balzac's *Un Début dans la vie*, Sérisy paradoxically violates the security and privacy of the postal system and simultaneously serves as an invisible agent to assure its security and privacy. He opens Georges Marest's satchel and steals a document, but it turns out to be his own document, and the theft is a successful attempt to prevent another theft, the real potential theft, the one he assumes Léger would eventually have committed.

There is more, however. It is significant that the count's discovery of the document representing him in a satchel in the coach is made at the first relay stop during the trip. Relays are crucial nodes along the system, because they are the places where information is concentrated and exchanged. Important messages circulate from relay to relay, and perspicacious travelers keep their ears open to hear whatever they can and to profit from these rich and complex points of exchange whenever possible. The second relay stop described by Balzac in the story confirms this observation in no uncertain terms. The innkeeper at the relay knows one of the passengers in Pierrotin's coach, namely, Léger, and, upon seeing him, asks him whether he has been able to secure Les Moulineaux for himself and to undo Sérisy's strategy. The innkeeper is well informed not only because he knows Léger but also, and most importantly, because the news of progress in the battle for Les Moulineaux has apparently traveled swiftly up and down the line between Paris and L'Isle-Adam: "But

François, the driver of the six o'clock Touchard coach, just told me that M. Margueron had been invited to dinner by Sérisy today at Presles" (1:796). Pierrotin shares the route with Touchard, but whether it be Pierrotin or a Touchard driver at the reins, everyone knows everything about what is happening along this itinerary.[13] In his essay on the English mail coach to which I have already referred, De Quincey reminds his reader that the coaches were thrilling not only because they were the fastest means of communication during the period, but also because they were heralds of national and international news disseminated along their routes by the coachmen and passengers, who informed people about the breaking news in the towns along the way as the journey progressed: "But the grandest chapter of our experience, within the whole mail-coach service, was on those occasions when we went down from London with the news of victory. A period of about ten years stretched from Trafalgar to Waterloo . . . [and] furnished a long succession of victories. . . . Five years of life it was worth paying down for the privilege of an outside place on a mail-coach, when carrying down the first tidings of any such event" (4:309–10). Whether it be national or international news, or simply the local gossip, information traveled faster than ever before along the system of relay stations. The conversation between the innkeeper and Léger is closely monitored by Sérisy, and from it he gleans a good deal more about the situation into which he is heading. Specifically, the exchange confirms that his *régisseur,* the administrator of his country estate at Presles, is in league with his enemies: "The count did not miss a single word of this hushed conversation. 'I have found proof here of what I was going to look for when I arrived'" (1:797).

One of the most striking elements of this initial narrative sequence is Pierrotin's investment in protecting and furthering Sérisy's strategy while transporting him to Presles. Pierrotin manages the way the intersection between passengers and information occurs in the course of the trip. He becomes the count's ally and protects his identity, never revealing it to the other travelers during the journey, because the count has promised him a handsome tip in exchange for this favor. After Sérisy overhears the conversation between Léger and the innkeeper, after he gauges the depth of the opposition to his purchase of Les Moulineaux and the care he must exercise to overcome it, he understands even more profoundly that his actions must be swift and hidden from his enemies. The immediate result of this discovery is that he ups the ante with Pierrotin. Pierrotin has ordered a new carriage, but he is a thousand francs short of the purchase price. Unless he comes up with the remaining sum within a short time (a day or two), he is going to lose his down payment entirely and miss the opportunity to replace his coach with a modern, more comfortable model. Sérisy thus appeals to Pierrotin in the strongest possible terms by directly addressing his business interests: "'Pierrotin,' he said in a soft voice to the stagecoach owner as he approached him, 'I promised you ten *louis* if you kept my secret; but if you continue to hide my name, . . . when you come by tomorrow morning I'll give you the thousand francs you need to pay for your new coach" (1:798). The structural logic of the initial sequence in *Un Début dans la vie* comes full circle here. The mode of conveyance used during the trip to L'Isle-Adam (Pierrotin's coach and its projected replacement by a brand-new model) as well as the intersection between the transportation of passengers and the exchange of information described in detail in the novel's early moments become the very object of the success of Pierrotin's evening run. They will result in the purchase Pierrotin must complete. Pierrotin is seeking confirmation that his grip on the region's transportation needs can expand.

The ultimate success of the count's financial operation signals simultaneously the success of Pierrotin's own transaction. The count's identity is indeed not revealed until the proper moment, and Pierrotin obtains the money to complete the purchase of his new coach. All of this is confirmed ironically by the novel's ending, which hammers the point home in spades. The conclusion brings the reader back to yet another trip along the route between Paris and L'Isle-Adam. This time Pierrotin and four of the travelers who rode with him during the first trip find themselves back together (Georges Marest, Oscar Husson, Joseph Bridau, and Léger), and Balzac draws the lessons from the story some fifteen years after the novel's opening scene. He multiplies the signs of Pierrotin's economic ascension. The coach in question is now one of the most modern and largest models, drawn by four horses instead of the two used at the beginning of the novel. It is a coach and horses "that would have made the Messageries Royales proud," the Messageries Royales being one of the two largest stagecoach companies of the period (the other was Laffitte and Caillard) (1:879). This is no longer the *voiture de Pierrotin,* but rather, *L'Hirondelle de l'Oise, hirondelle* meaning "swallow," a fast-flying bird and thus a name that calls attention to the coach service's speed. Pierrotin is holding his own on this local route, like the local coaches that are prospering on the Versailles route in the face of competition from the railroad (to which Balzac here refers once again [1:879]). His line now has an official mail contract, as the narrator indicates when he remarks that Pierrotin is keeping an eye on the work of "two postmen in uniform who were loading numerous packages on the vast top deck of his coach" (1:879). His clientele is now of the highest quality, moreover, as Georges

Marest observes when he discovers that only one seat remains for the trip: "It seems that whatever government is in power, the French peers travel in Pierrotin's coaches" (1:881). Léger is identified as a double millionaire by the narrator, and the loquacious Georges finally sums up Pierrotin's position: "Pierrotin now is the sole owner of the transport company of the Oise Valley [that is, he has succeeded in pushing aside his strong competitor of the previous decade, Touchard], and he has very nice coaches. . . . He is a bourgeois from Beaumont, where he has a hotel in which the stagecoach passengers stay. He has a wife and daughter who are quite respectable" (1:882).

Pierrotin has succeeded at least as well as Minoret-Levrault in *Ursule Mirouët,* although he has understood better than Minoret-Levrault that the future of road transportation belongs to the companies running the coaches and not to the *maîtres de poste.* The latter are nearly at the end of their economic boom as railroad construction begins, whereas an entrepreneur like Pierrotin, whose skill is in organizing a whole business, will have the potential to adapt as the economic transformations gain momentum. Oscar Husson, whose ignorance and lack of perspicacity during the first trip recounted in the novel almost ruined his career, shows his signature imbecility once again, when he treats Pierrotin as if he were the same person he was years earlier during the first trip: "'Poor old Pierrotin, . . . like me, he has not gotten very far in life. . . . Let's dine together here, Pierrotin,' said Oscar loudly as he slapped the transporter's back" (1:886). To which Pierrotin responds, "I'm not the driver. . . . [I'm] the owner" (1:886). Balzac punishes Oscar for this last miscalculation—if not too harshly, nonetheless quite ironically. In the closing lines, the narrator indicates that Oscar has married Pierrotin's daughter, who brings a substantial dowry to the wedding: "Two months after moving to Beaumont-sur-Oise, Oscar was courting Mlle. Georgette Pierrotin, whose dowry was one hundred fifty thousand francs, and he married the daughter of the owner of the Oise transportation company toward the end of the winter of 1838" (1:877). The contrast between the beginning and the ending of the novel, then, allows Balzac to use the example of Pierrotin to chronicle graphically the rise of larger and consolidated coach transportation companies, which regularized overland travel in France during the Restoration and the July Monarchy and were built on the principles of increased precision and speed developed in the first half of the nineteenth century in Western Europe and the United States. Simultaneously, however, Balzac suggests that the relative openness of Pierrotin's beginnings, when he had a certain flexibility to negotiate in the interstices of the system, has given way to a rationalization analogous to the closing down of the social space indicated by the novel's last sentence describing Oscar Husson's final success: "He has finally become the modern bourgeois" (1:887).[14]

Let us shift our attention from *Un Début dans la vie* and its focus on the concentration of bourgeois power through increasing organization—reflected in the successful growth of Pierrotin's coach company—toward the earliest novel Balzac composed of those included in *La Comédie humaine, Les Chouans.*[15] The novel begins *in medias res,* and that narrative middle is marked by a journey. The fact that beginning in the middle simultaneously means beginning in the middle of a journey is of crucial importance for understanding the novel and will present yet another occasion to demonstrate how fundamental the themes of travel and rapid movement were for Balzac from the very beginning of the project of *La Comédie humaine.* The republican soldiers Balzac describes in the initial scene have interrupted their march on the road between the towns of Fougères and Mayenne in Brittany. Balzac's treatment of this moment and his later development of the themes and structures present in it suggest that we can describe *Les Chouans,* at least in part, as a vast meditation on space, communication, and strategy, in which movement—the speed and efficiency with which it takes place—is paramount. One might readily claim that the novel describes the construction of a veritable strategic machine, conceived to entrap adversaries, to corner them, and eventually to kill them by mobilizing a certain perspective on movements and the strategies associated with them. Political and police machinations and military machines coalesce in the novel to describe a new regime, a postrevolutionary one in which certain kinds of communication become principal elements. *Les Chouans* demonstrates just how conscious Balzac had become of characteristic outcomes to which the revolutionary moment had led. It would be helpful to begin a discussion of the novel by contextualizing *Les Chouans,* because it is not the best known or most widely read of the texts in *La Comédie humaine.* It was first published in 1829, and the preface to the novel clearly indicates the extent to which it was an experimental and transitional narrative, one in which Balzac began a conscious quest for a style that would move him away from the structures and modes of presentation characteristic of the stories he had composed before the project of *La Comédie humaine* began to take shape. In *Les Chouans,* he was beginning to formulate a perspective on history that would permit him to rethink the bases of the historical novel à la Walter Scott.

The main lines of the story in the novel are as follows: An armed republican contingent, sent by the first consul, Napoleon Bonaparte, has been given the order to crush an antirevolutionary revolt, a *chouannerie* as it is called in the novel and was called during the historical period in question, organized by the Breton peasants. Colonel Hulot, a hardened and experienced battle veteran of the revolutionary wars, is pitted against the marquis de Montauran, better know in the novel by his nickname, le Gars, who is commanding the Breton rebels. Hulot is aided and abetted—and later superseded against his will and better judgment—by a secret agent of the first consul, a courtesan, Marie de Verneuil, sent to the region by the minister of police, the infamous Fouché, in order to seduce Montauran, capture him, and remove his leadership from the royalist peasant revolt. Marie de Verneuil will in turn be seconded by Corentin, another of Fouché's secret agents, sent to keep an eye on Marie herself. The presence in the novel of Marie de Verneuil and Corentin and the complex relations between the two of them, as well as their function as secret agents, are from the start unmistakable signs that clear-cut military confrontations between opposing forces respecting the "rules" of war (if indeed there have ever been such rules) are a thing of the past. In this novel, we are already in a military modernity of propaganda, trickery, secrecy, in short, of a sustained illegality in which the policing military forces are as bad as, if not worse than, the brigands they attempt to control. As Balzac remarks: "If the Vendée turned brigandage into war, Brittany turned war into brigandage" (*Les Chouans* 8:919).

The characters in the story will be called upon to exercise uncommon perspicacity while navigating the shifting and extraordinarily complex spatial grounds of this guerrilla war. The short journey described in the opening pages of the novel has been undertaken by a contingent of republican soldiers who are escorting a group of Breton peasants called up in a general conscription designed to recruit new soldiers for the dirty war that is under way. Balzac takes up the story at a moment when the republican soldiers have interrupted their march on the road between the towns of Fougères and Mayenne. One of the unwilling conscripts, Marche-à-Terre, later identified as an important officer in the rebel army, has provoked a disruption in the march that has led to a halt, and that halt will in turn become an ambush. Not only are we in the middle of a journey as the novel begins, but we are also stopped, blocked on the road in a traffic jam. Traffic problems that interrupt circulation and enable military ambushes are profoundly linked in *Les Chouans.* Just before the ambush occurs, however, the interruption in the journey allows the soldiers to contemplate the town of Fougères from the heights of a mountain called

La Pèlerine (well named, since the word shares its root with the term "pilgrim") and therefore allows the narrator to describe the topography of the place where the events of the story are to occur: "From the summit of La Pèlerine, the great Couesnon Valley appears before the eyes of the traveler. One of its culminating points is occupied on the horizon by the town of Fougères. The town's château, perched on a rock formation upon which it is built, overlooks three or four important roads, a geographical position that in the past made it one of the keys to Brittany" (8:912).

On the one hand, the road, and on the other, the fortified town: What is the relation between the two? That relation takes on some complex resonances if one defines the town or city in a manner slightly skewed with respect to the traditional perspectives that have marked historical and sociological approaches to city structures. Paul Virilio suggests how such a change in perspective can affect the way one imagines what the city is in relation to the roads that lead to it and cross through it. Here is a key passage on this question from his *Vitesse et politique:*

> The city has not always been perceived as a human habitat penetrated by a rapid corridor of communication (river, road, shore, railroad . . .). The fact that the street is simply a road crossing through a conglomeration has often been forgotten—even though everyday laws governing the "speed limit" of vehicles in cities remind us of the continuousness of crossings and movements solely modulated by the law of speed. The city is but a halt, a point on the synoptical route of a trajectory, in ancient times a glacis [a slope extending down from a fortification], or a path at the crest of a hill or the top of a fortification, a border or a shore, where the human gaze and the speed of displacement of vehicles are instrumentally associated. (15–16)

Virilio focuses our attention on the notions of circulation and communication that are integral to the conception of the city. The economic opulence and the elaborate structures of modern cities (with their universities, museums, stores, and permanent cultural and social festivities) seem to give the city an appearance of permanence, the characteristics of a fixed point, a place of sojourn after long journeys, the very center of social urbanity. What has been forgotten, according to Virilio, is precisely the fact that the city is perhaps not a place of social and cultural exchange as much as it is an interchange in a road, a simple crossroads where routes intersect with one another. Provocatively, Virilio will suggest that what we have interpreted as social exchange might simply be circulation and control of that circulation by material and legal measures that have taken on the appearance of social relations, when, in fact, they are nothing more than the rules of the road.

The regulations concerning public spaces one finds in cities as early as the Middle Ages demonstrate this, Virilio maintains. Take, for example, the well-known fact that traditionally cities have taxed windows and façades on streets. Whatever other factors might be used to construct an explanation for this social and political phenomenon, one part of such an explanation must surely be that the interface between the emerging bourgeois domicile and routes of communication carries with it the possibility of negotiation, exchange, and information gathering. Windows and façades permit one to see what is happening in the street, ultimately to solicit clients, to establish a place from which one can create strategies of selling and exchanging goods, as well as information. A panoramic view on what is arriving and what is leaving is invaluable—the spectacle of the street connects the observer to the fluidity and mobility of movement along a road system that is the very definition of the social. Control of the speed of passage of goods, information, and people provides a means for what Virilio calls social progress, which always already means to be mobile and thus literally to progress.

The rearranging of the city in a way favorable to the needs of the first representatives of an emerging bourgeoisie began as early as the Middle Ages with certain advantages that allowed for primitive policing activities. A specific social group was able to begin occupying the space of the city in strategic ways, to solidify its hold, to establish itself with stability in the key parts of the city (precisely by means of acquiring *biens immobiliers,* as the French expression puts it so aptly, immobile, unmovable positions situated on the network of roads defining the city): "The bourgeoisie derives its initial power and class characteristics less from commerce and industry . . . than from a strategic implantation establishing the 'fixed domicile' as a value, . . . the right to reside within the ramparts of fortified towns" (*Vitesse* 18–19). These observations have a strong architectural subtext in Virilio's analyses. The transformation from the layout of the ancient Roman city into that of the fortified city was meant less to protect citizens from war machines (catapults and later cannons) than to control the circulation of soldiers—as well as that of migratory waves of foreigners, who threatened periodically to overrun cities. The architectural plan of fortified cities is not designed simply to turn invaders back at the outer walls. Thanks to a careful organization of interior spaces, the fortified city succeeds in indefinitely prolonging the space of combat—with openings, unpredictable zigzags, walls, and labyrinths of all sorts. The city absorbs combatants, who arrive within its boundaries possessed of a formidable destructive energy, by dispersing and thus dissipating their energy (19–20). Fortified cities should be analyzed as interchanges, as means of directing circulation in order to reduce it to less dangerous and destructive levels and forms. Is the system of beltways around modern cities not a modern version of this, partially functioning as a circulatory buffer of sorts? One does not enter into a modern city as one wishes and where one wishes, but only along the lines and through the interchanges that have been designated as the entry points—and only at the speeds dictated by regulations.

In the beginning of *Les Chouans,* when the republican forces stop on the road in a place that gives them a full view of what is below, they see the fortified town of Fougères opposite them at the end of the valley. As the story progresses, this town will become a veritable war machine in the sense that Virilio defines it. It will be the center of a machination against the Breton rebels that will eventually entrap them, absorb the energy of their movement (like quicksand), and end the uprising. Indeed, Marie de Verneuil, Napoleon's agent sent to seduce and ultimately to capture the leader of the peasant uprising, will live in Fougères in a house situated in a manner that recognizes the underlying nature of the town's topography. The building is nestled in the very fortifications that protect the town: "At the place where the public avenue ends at the town's fortifications is a tower called the Tower of Papegaut. Starting at the level of this square construction, upon which was built the house in which Mlle. de Verneuil lived, there are walls or rock formations wherever the rock is flat enough" (8:1070–71). It is an extension of those fortifications and thus an integral part of the labyrinth that controls and directs the flow of people in and through Fougères. Marie can observe the comings and goings of those who pass through. Her situation prepares her to assert political domination through the control of circulatory patterns in a manner corresponding quite strikingly to Virilio's analyses. Moreover, her fellow conspirator, Corentin, the police agent charged with making sure she accomplishes her mission, is, it goes almost without saying, the one who discovered this extraordinarily appropriate dwelling for savvy political and military strategists. At the end of the novel, at the moment when preparations for the final ambush to entrap Montauran are complete, Marie's house will be at the heart of the deployment of republican forces occupying key points of the town's labyrinthine interior. To await the prey in the chicanes of the fortified town is the exemplary military operation: one must impose speed limits if one wants to exercise political power. The trap laid for Montauran within the maze of streets and routes that composes Fougères is architecturally so powerful that Marie's change of heart, when she decides she wants to save him from the Revolution, is not sufficient to extricate him from danger. Along with Marie, he is caught in the complexities of the topography in Fougères, ultimately immobilized in the knots of the web that has been prepared by the republicans.

The narrative in the first pages of the novel juxtaposes the road leading from Fougères toward Mayenne and the fortified town of Fougères and incorporates both into a topology of circulation—of troops, goods, and information. As Virilio would suggest, the political power of the state is only secondarily the organized oppression of one class by another; it is first and foremost, and in a very material way, the act of policing a road system. In a lapidary formula Virilio describes the Revolution as "a riot with its traffic jams, illegal parking, fender benders, and collisions" (*Vitesse* 23–24). The halt in the progress of the republican troops on the heights of La Pèlerine, at first apparently a touristic interlude of contemplation, is also simultaneously a traffic jam that presents a mortal danger. It is an interruption to the free, efficient, and quick movement of the soldiers from one town to another and thus the perfect place for an ambush to occur. At crucial points where interruptions of this sort arise in *Les Chouans,* fundamental dangers always lurk. Marche-à-Terre, whose name is clearly symptomatic of certain elements in our argument, consciously provokes a delay in the military march at the top of La Pèlerine to expose the republican troops to the rebel forces, who can threaten the republicans only in a moment of immobility.

The flip side of this first ambush scene is a scene that follows immediately, during which the Breton rebels abandon their confrontation with the republican soldiers in order to ambush and rob a coach making its way along the same road. This incident is the second half of a symbolic diptych—on the one hand, the interrupted march that turns into an ambush, on the other, the robbing of a coach along the same road. The novel begins on the road and remains there resolutely in its introductory sequences. The coach in question is called a *turgotine* by the narrator. The name comes from the founder of the centralized system of public coaches, Turgot, whose contribution to the reorganization of overland travel has already been briefly described. There is a double irony here. First, the term *turgotine* was coined by the enemies of Turgot, who used it to ridicule him and ultimately to run him out office within a year after his reform, because they resisted the changes in coach travel that had been sought by his intervention. Second, Balzac takes comic pleasure in using the term, because the coach is not actually a *turgotine:* it is one of the vehicles remaining from the old coach network, relegated to this backward and underdeveloped province. In particular, it does not have the suspension system of the new *diligences* (stagecoaches) and resembles a sort of elaborate oxcart rather than the modern conveyances from which it is usurping its name. The stopping of this coach by the Breton rebels is the second consecutive occurrence in the novel of a policing activity along what is clearly a crucial artery between Fougères and Mayenne. The Breton irregulars demonstrate their strategic superiority in the region by imposing their control along the road in place of the republican forces, literally in nearly the exact same location from which they have just dislodged the republicans during the ambush with which the novel begins.

There is more. Marie de Verneuil herself is on the move when we first encounter her later in the novel. Colonel Hulot meets her coach on the way to Alençon while he is on patrol some time after the opening ambush. Marie is immediately referred to in the text as *la voyageuse,* the traveler. In the course of the journey that she has undertaken to bring her into the fray and to initiate her strategy to find and entrap the rebel leader, she actually meets that leader, Montauran, for the first time. It happens that Montauran is traveling under an assumed identity along the same route. But this narrative coincidence is clearly more than coincidental if seen in light of the law of movement that governs the novel from the opening pages. The two characters meet in a tavern at a relay along the road Marie has taken to get to Fougères. We have already seen how crucial relays are when it comes to questions of information exchange and communication. Montauran invites her to eat dinner with him and his companion, and later the conversation continues as he joins her in her coach, now escorted by a group of republican soldiers. In the course of the next leg of her journey, she has one of her most frank conversations with Montauran, although she is unable to confirm her suspicions concerning his identity. At one point during this part of the journey, the two travelers get out of the coach to walk alongside it while climbing a steep grade in the road going over the mountain, La Pèlerine, that is the scene of the ambush with which the novel begins. The journey becomes the site of a lovers' promenade. This is proof, of course, that in the scene we are not yet really in the domain of the fully developed public transportation system initiated by the experiment of the *turgotine,* because the characteristic of that system as it later materialized during the 1830s was precisely that it finally brought the velocity of coaches to a level in excess of the speed of walking and put an end to the hybrid experience (both riding and walking) that characterized earlier coach travel. As Christophe Studeny has put it in his essay on the invention of speed in France: "The new *diligence* produced a break in the [understanding of] proximity by regularly exceeding the threshold of the speed possible for a man on foot" (79). The clichéd scene of lovers walking beside a vehicle whose speed does not exceed theirs and thus allows them to have a private conversation—even though they find themselves in a public conveyance—can be found regularly in narratives of the first decades of the nineteenth century. A variation on it, for example, occurs in the first half of Stendhal's *Lucien Leuwen*, when Lucien talks with Mme. de Chasteller while walking behind a carriage returning from the café *Le Chasseur vert*.

Virtually everyone in *Les Chouans* is on the move, in transit, trying to get somewhere else in the quickest and most efficient manner—at least until Marie settles into her fortress/house in Fougères. The first chance encounter between Marie de Verneuil and Montauran in the course of their respective journeys gives Marie a chance to protect him, thereby creating an obligation that immediately binds them together. Even if Marie cannot confirm his identity during their conversation, enough suspicion remains to warrant an arrest, especially during this revolutionary period of unrest and rebellion. One word from her would make of him an immediate candidate for the guillotine. Her aristocratic gesture of honor in choosing to protect Montauran betrays her budding fascination with him. Its immediate effect, in any case, is to oblige him profoundly enough so that, in turn, in order to protect her when the coach in which they are riding comes under threat of attack by the Breton rebels during the night, he invites her to a rustic château in the region that serves as the center of *chouan* military operations, La Vivetière. No one travels on the roads around Mayenne and Fougères without living under the threat of a traffic jam in the form of an ambush. Unfortunately for Marie—but quite logically in the story—the sanctuary against danger proposed by Montauran, La Vivetière, is yet another space of blockage and ambush, and the republican troops accompanying Marie's coach must bear the consequences when they are attacked and decimated by the rebels while at La Vivetière. One must ultimately argue that Balzac's *Les Chouans* is constructed on a trope of opposition between Fougères, the republican fortified encampment, and La Vivetière, stronghold of the rebels. It would seem at first glance that these two places resemble one another—both are locations for ambushes of any oppositional forces unhappy enough to pass by too closely. But nothing would be more misleading than to remain at this level of superficial resemblance. Key differences mark the two geographical spaces. La Vivetière is isolated, set off outside the network of communication represented by the road system upon which so much of the novel takes place. It is located at the extreme limits of a dead end, surrounded by water and bogs. Only one road leads into it, a road that ends in a muddy morass that strangely resembles the state of the unkempt roads of a previous era during the rainy season and that blocks all further circulation. Separated from the road network, La Vivetière is the utter opposite of a crossroads or an interchange—it is much more like a Bermuda Triangle. The republican troops are massacred there almost by accident, as if they had momentarily forgotten that their destiny is not to go down a dead end, not to be shunted down a siding off the main road, but, on the contrary, to extend their march, in an act of circulation indefinitely prolonged—the very essence of their role as conscripts in that great general conscription that began during the Terror in 1793. The comparison between La Vivetière and Fougères highlights these issues eloquently: Fougères is a place of intersection of three or four major routes, as it is first described in the novel—it is one of the keys to travel in and out of Brittany. Its location is thus explicitly opposed to La Vivetière's geographical situation. La Vivetière is a dead spot on the map of Brittany and thus, by extension, a place of backwardness removed from the Revolution, especially if one characterizes the Revolution as a "movement" in the Virilian sense. The space and circulation of the bourgeois town of Fougères allow for speed of passage and its modulation. What the new group of governors of Fougères, the republicans, must construct is a regime that permits and polices the circulation of people, goods, and armies, that connects this backward region to the Revolution, to a new France on the move.

This brings us back momentarily to the first scene in the novel at the summit of Le Pèlerine. Its structure contains not only the opposition—and now we must also say the complex connection—between the road and the town but a third element as well, one that was glossed over without underscoring its significance in a first reading of the novel's opening scenes, namely, the conscription of the citizens of the region into the republican army, into its mission on the march. The goal of the forced march at the beginning of the novel was to accompany newly conscripted Bretons to Mayenne to fulfill the formalities of enrolling them in the army. The importance of the notion of conscription that underlies the scene is not accidental. If one thinks for a moment about the nature of that conscription, it quickly becomes a key symptomatic element in understanding the opening scene and the novel as a whole. Virilio's remarks on conscription during the Revolution make the issues at stake here vivid:

> The new organization of the flow of circulation that has been arbitrarily called the French Revolution . . . is but the rational organization of a social abduction. The "general conscription" [*levée en masse*] of 1793 is the *kidnapping of the masses*. . . . While [the bourgeoisie] stayed home and acquired new properties, new buildings and houses, . . . what that

> same bourgeoisie offered *as land to these soldiers called up by decree of the Convention were the roads of Europe.* "Wherever the feet are, there is the fatherland" (*ubi pedes, ibi patria*), as Roman law had already put it. With the French Revolution, *all roads became national!*[16] (*Vitesse* 29, Virilio's italics)

The revolutionary armies, composed for the most part of the poorest and most powerless citizens, were sent out on the road to defend the nation and to conquer Europe in the name of the principles of the Revolution. What better means of preventing them from contesting the pillage of public property accomplished by those left behind in the capital? And if Hulot, the wizened old revolutionary at the head of the republican forces at the beginning of Balzac's novel, is destined to be left behind by the events that occur around him during the rebellion, it is because this inveterate traveler, *vieux routier de la Révolution,* as the expression would go in French, realizes that the true chicane (in the sense of zigzag as well as in the sense of chicanery) is in the town—where roads intersect, where interchanges are constructed, where political power is constituted by an ever more sophisticated policing of circulation. The person destined to replace Hulot, Corentin, already knows that what circulates on this new road system are no longer the colors of the Revolution, *la cocarde,* but instead the state secrets of a new secret police, a police traveling the roads with eyes and ears open for the rumors spread by a citizenry well schooled by the Revolution in the tactics of denunciation and betrayal of neighbors and friends.

If *Les Chouans* is indeed characterized by communicational networks in the form of roads, it is marked as well by messengers who crisscross and inhabit those roads. Within the configuration of intersecting trajectories meticulously described in the novel, messages are exchanged, beginning with the whistles and bird calls that signal the attack by *chouan* forces crowning the first narrative sequence of the novel and continuing throughout the various stages of the strategy that leads to the capture of Montauran. Marie de Verneuil carries a letter destined for republican commanders in Brittany to inform them that she has jurisdiction over them. Corentin, who accompanies Marie, is the bearer of secret instructions unknown to Marie. Additionally, in the culminating sequence of the novel, Corentin gives instructions to Hulot that run counter to the secret messages exchanged between Marie and Montauran. Ultimately, the republican soldiers must also be seen as messengers, as incessantly moving travelers, who spread the word of the republic wherever they go. Everywhere in the novel characters are attempting to contact one another, to exchange information, and to understand each other's strategies by somehow stealing messages destined for adversaries. This is perhaps the most troubling aspect of an approach to the novel that adopts the perspective of communication. We cannot speak of transparency in *Les Chouans,* no matter how established, complex, and complete the circuits in the network of exchanges may be. If anything, *Les Chouans* is a novel of deception. It is also a novel in which Balzac shows that the last stages of the political upheaval provoked by the Revolution are an operation conceived and implemented by the secret police of the first consul. When Hulot resigns his command upon discovering that he is outranked by Marie de Verneuil, his act denotes the end of republican military virtues and the beginning of a new regime in which honesty and ethical openness have no place. The circuits of communication in the novel are created seemingly not to exchange information openly but rather to send secrets and to conceal intentions.

The way Corentin travels around the countryside in *Les Chouans* looking for information bears a strange resemblance to a favorite police tactic applied once the railroad system was in place later in the century, namely, riding the rails on the prowl for suspicious-looking characters or deeds. Speed in moving people and information is constantly linked to policing in the nineteenth century. A short anecdote from a moment nearly fifty years after the events recounted in *Les Chouans* confirms this observation. In England in 1845, the usefulness of the electrical telegraph for people other than railroad personnel trying to operate trains on time was given exemplary proof. A telegraph operator up the line from Paddington Station sent ahead a description of a murderer who had gotten on a train and escaped the town in which the murder was committed. When the train arrived in Paddington, the police were there to arrest the murderer immediately, because they had been given his exact description in advance. This is one of the first recorded uses of the telegraph for nonrailroad purposes in England. Fittingly, it is directly related to policing a subject in movement. Corentin is a distant predecessor of the plainclothes detectives of the second half of the century, and we shall have occasion to encounter him again in another of Balzac's novels, *Une Ténébreuse affaire,* about which I shall have more to say, because it is another locus of Balzacian reflection on travel and communication.

For now, however, our observations concerning Balzac's intelligent understanding of road travel and topography can be extended further. If Balzac got the description of the relationship between road and town right in *Les Chouans,* we must also remember that he was very perspicacious when it came to understanding the complexities of streets and spaces in the capital itself, in Paris. It would not be farfetched to describe Eugène de Rastignac's social and cultural education in *Le Père Goriot* as a mapping of the city space of Paris that will allow him to understand social relations in a spatial way that is impossible as the novel begins. The layout of urban routes is an essential source of information that he must explore and understand coherently if he is to succeed socially and ultimately to assert himself in the circles of society that will give him the most direct access to power. As readers of *Le Père Goriot* know, Rastignac lives in a room rented in Mme. Vauquer's boardinghouse during the events recounted in the novel, and the location of the boardinghouse in the city's street network is a significant starting point for a reflection on Rastignac's social progress. The rue Neuve-Sainte-Geneviève is between the Latin Quarter and the Faubourg Saint-Marceau, which is only marginally a part of the city.[17] In fact, the rue Neuve-Sainte-Geneviève is a border space between the city and its outside, even though the area within which the street is located can technically be called a neighborhood of the city. For all intents and purposes, it is impracticable for vehicular circulation: "The boardinghouse . . . stands at the lower end of the rue Neuve-Sainte-Geneviève where it slopes so abruptly toward the rue de l'Arbalète that carriages rarely use it."[18] The neighborhood of the rue Neuve-Sainte-Geneviève strangely resembles what in French would be termed a *banlieue,* a neighborhood that is at a certain distance from the city (*lieue*), but that is linked to it in specific legal ways (*ban*), in other words, a tributary of the city that is not actually a part of it.

One way of describing the problem that confronts Rastignac as the novel opens would be to say that he must learn how to penetrate the space of the city's center, the heart of its social life, how to understand Parisian topography from the vantage point of the ill-defined space of the socioeconomic *banlieue* to which he is initially confined. Since the rue Neuve-Sainte-Geneviève is only tenuously related to the city, the passage from this neighborhood to other neighborhoods is difficult—it will require a sustained effort to grasp a complex set of relationships that are the real object of Rastignac's act of mapping. The literal and symbolic distance his topographical education covers during the novel is strongly foregrounded by the story's final sequence. Intersected by a thematics of space and connections that repeats the opening pages, the novel's concluding passage reworks the initial sequence. Specifically, it takes place in a very different—a consciously different—space. Rastignac attends the pauper's burial of Goriot in the Père Lachaise Cemetery accompanied only by Mme. Vauquer's domestic servant Christophe and eventually by servants from the Restaud and Nucingen households—both families send empty carriages to mark their absent participation. At the end of the service, as every reader of Balzac knows, Rastignac has a full view of the city's center from this elevated point. The panorama elaborated in the description encompasses the entire skyline and allows Rastignac's gaze to plunge into the heart of the city as never before, to see its essence. The new perspective described contrasts starkly with the closed, closeted vision to which Rastignac had been limited in the street where Mme. Vauquer's boardinghouse is located. Now endowed with a more inclusive and penetrating vision of the city's organization attained through a process of symbolic mapping that has required him to circulate through the streets of various neighborhoods in the city, he can make his famous remark: "A nous deux maintenant" (3:290).

Just how does one get from the first of these places to the other? For Rastignac, to learn the city space means to map it, at least in part, by walking in it. A fundamental activity of his apprenticeship is to navigate the city on foot. At first glance, this might appear to be a rather simple statement. One must not, however, underestimate its theoretical significance. Specifically, one must call attention to the differences between the act of moving in a given space while in a conveyance and the act of moving in that same space on foot. The insight into the detail of a terrain that one obtains by exploring its irregularities on foot has little common measure with the knowledge that one gathers when enclosed in a carriage, for instance. Transportation by vehicle depends entirely on the fact that the space in question has been rearranged into a costly and constraining infrastructure. A network of streets has the effect of carefully directing and limiting the way one can move about in the city. The passenger is ultimately a prisoner of the vehicle and is therefore confined to an officially sanctioned network already laid out by urban authorities. The possibility of making aleatory connections, of working toward a deeper understanding of the complexity of the landscape is precluded under such circumstances. Jean-Marc Lévy-Leblond sums up these points succinctly. While his perspective is modern, the lesson can easily be transposed to the period in Balzac's novel:

> No doubt planes, trains, and automobiles go faster than the walker. But have we really understood the extreme limitations they impose on the trips we take? Their effectiveness comes at a price, namely, a heavy and restrictive infrastructure. A few airports or railroad tracks, a network of highways will never cover more than an infinitesimal portion of the planet. Wherever you go, you will finish your trip on foot. In bed, at the ta-

ble, on the beach, in the middle of the forest, only your body will reach its goal. (39)

What Lévy-Leblond underlines here and what is suggestive in the case of Rastignac is the importance of the body's kinetic displacement in space as a device for understanding the detail of the terrain in which one is moving. Michel de Certeau said much the same thing when he wrote of the paths and trajectories of the walker in the modern cityscape: "History begins at ground level, with footsteps. They are numerous, but they do not fit together to create a series. They cannot be counted, because each one is qualitative, a style of tactile comprehension and kinetic appropriation. Their teeming multitude makes up innumerable singularities. Their play does not fashion space. They weave together places" (179). The subtleties of the links, passages, bridges of the Parisian cityscape cannot be understood in quite the same way by a passenger in a vehicle. The relationship between the routes taken by a vehicle in rapid movement and the slower, more aleatory routes of the walker is explored by Balzac through the description of Rastignac's progression in *Le Père Goriot*. Those routes do more, in fact, than simply create a map comparable to a city map like those bought in a tourist shop. They weave together places in the urban space, that is, they allow the walker to transform the city into a comprehensible and usable tactical diagram for action, creating knowledge about what group is linked to another—no matter how complex the network.

It is no easy task to figure out the shortcuts and short circuits of the city. Areas that do not seem to be in the vicinity of one another nevertheless are in surprising proximity at certain crucial moments—in a process that is almost like the topological problem of the "baker's transformation" in mathematics. Imagine a piece of dough that has been flattened and is then folded and flattened again in a series of regular operations, bringing points marked at various places on the surface of the dough into the vicinity of one another in increasingly complex and aleatory ways. Rastignac's topographical education quickly becomes a topological one, thanks to the complexities of the city space. A striking example of unexpected vicinities occurs early in the novel, on the morning after Rastignac has attended his first ball at Mme. de Beauséant's residence. In the neighborhood of Mme. Vauquer's boardinghouse, he espies Anastasie de Restaud, to whom he was introduced at the ball. The appearance of the elegant countess in surroundings that are utterly removed from the region where she normally lives is extremely surprising. A desire immediately arises to discover what bridge connects the Faubourg Saint-Germain to the area around the rue Neuve-Sainte-Geneviève: "Was it not strange to meet one of the prettiest women in Paris in the rue des Grès at nine o'clock, when she could not have come from the ball before two in the morning? It's only in Paris you meet with such adventures," comments Rastignac (3:87). A bridge connects spatial varieties that are unrelated. Before the bridge was constructed, there was no way to get from one to the other, and yet once that bridge exists, crossing it creates a new hybrid space.[19]

Not only did Anastasie venture into a sector of the city far-removed from her usual neighborhood, but when Rastignac sees her, she is on foot—surely not something to be expected of a wealthy and apparently powerful woman. The peculiar short circuit between one part of the city and another that occurs here is inexplicable. Rastignac is simply not yet prepared to understand it. Not surprisingly, the key to the enigma belongs to Vautrin, who, although he does not provide a full explanation, hints that he understands the nature of the bridge in question: "'Yesterday dancing at a Duchess's ball,' said Vautrin, 'this morning visiting a money-lender; from the highest arc of fortune's wheel to the bottom of the social ladder: behold the progress of Parisian women!'" (3:87). The more experienced geographer in the story at this point is obviously Vautrin. His knowledge and expertise are emblematically represented by the fact that only he possesses a passkey to the Vauquer boardinghouse. His ability to come and go as he pleases at any hour of the day or night demonstrates the extent to which he has free run not only of the space of the Vauquer household but also, by extension, of the city with which this domestic space communicates. Open doors lead to other doors, to bridges, to connections that Vautrin has thoroughly explored, about which he has constructed a veritable theory, in fact.

Another highly emblematic sequence in the novel that combines the problem of mapping and the need to move on foot in order to grasp the complexities of urban territories is the description of the first and only visit Rastignac makes to Anastasie de Restaud's house. After dressing in his finest clothes, he sets out toward her neighborhood on foot—with predictable results:

> Eugène walked with a thousand precautions against splashing himself with mud, but with his mind wholly fixed on what he would say to Mme. de Restaud. He laid in a stock of wit; he invented scintillating retorts to the imaginary remarks; he prepared his polished lines, his phrases in the style of Talleyrand, for imaginary situations favorable to the declaration on which he was to found his future. And so he became spattered with mud after all, poor student, and was forced to have his shoes polished and his breeches brushed at the Palais-Royal.

> "If I were rich," he said to himself as he changed a five-franc piece that he had brought *in case of need,* "I should have gone by cab, then I could have thought at my leisure." (3:94, Balzac's italics)

Perhaps Rastignac would have been able to think more clearly about the anticipated conversation had he taken a cab, but the trip is more than an occasion for inventing witty repartee; it is also the experience of a route, a necessary prospecting of the itinerary between his living quarters and the aristocratic neighborhood in which the Hôtel de Restaud is to be found. The practical difficulties that Rastignac encounters—mud and the necessity of cleaning it off his clothing—are not extraneous, but central. A carriage might have spared his shoes and pants, but it would not have allowed him to fill in essential details to the indispensable map of the city he is formulating through the experience of prospecting passages.

The scene demonstrates, moreover, that the topographical problem of transition between the Vauquer pension and the Restaud residence hides another set of complexities—the first problem is doubled by a second one, namely, the transition between the street and the Restaud household itself. Obliged to cross the courtyard on foot, Rastignac becomes the butt of the servants' jokes, because the domestics in the household are used to visitors who arrive only in the most stylish carriages. The awkwardness of Rastignac's entry is a prelude to his failure within the house, where he immediately betrays his ignorance of the layout of the rooms, that is, of the interior topography, and ends up crossing through the service rooms while attempting to enter the parlor. Decidedly, Rastignac has a lot to learn about spatial relations. The first part of the scene in the Restaud household ends, moreover, with Rastignac looking out the window and beholding the courtyard through which he just walked and in which, to his surprise, he espies another visitor on foot: Goriot. Rastignac, who does not yet know of the filial relationship between Goriot and Anastasie de Restaud, catches sight of Goriot just as the old man is leaving after having visited his daughter. Goriot's appearance in this context is both surprising and mysterious to Rastignac. How is it that the space between the Vauquer household, where Goriot lives, and the Restaud household can be connected? How can an obscure inhabitant from one of the spaces be transported into the other? The question applies to Rastignac himself as well as to Goriot, and Rastignac's inability to grasp how this transport is possible is precisely what leads to the social faux pas that will permanently close the door of the Restaud household to him: Rastignac mentions Goriot to the count Restaud. The reversal of perspective that occurs in the scene, moreover, prefigures the reversal that characterizes the novel's final scene. Rastignac is plunged into the space of the

Restaud courtyard without any perspective possible—everyone, including the servants of the household, has the advantage and is thus able to adopt an ironic stance toward his behavior. Once within the house and able to look back at the courtyard, however, Rastignac sees someone like himself (old Goriot) and immediately assumes a position of perspectivist mastery with respect to this other person. Unhappily for Rastignac, the reversal of perspective in this case is premature. He is unable to use it, to understand it, and is, therefore, unable to transform it into a strategy. In fact, his attempt to mobilize his fleeting superiority over Goriot by mentioning their acquaintance is precisely what leads to Rastignac's ultimate downfall in the Restaud household.

If this sequence can be considered archetypal for Rastignac's mapping attempts at grasping itineraries created by walking, experiences obtained through other means of transportation make important appearances as well in the narrative and contribute to the portrait of Rastignac's social ignorance. Bitter over his defeat in the Restaud household, Rastignac impulsively hails a cab that takes him to see his cousin, Mme. de Beauséant. This episode contains, then, both a trip on foot and one in a carriage. The carriage portion holds yet another lesson and a considerable dose of irony. On asking to be taken to the Hôtel de Beauséant, Rastignac is informed that his request is ambiguous:

> "Where to, sir?" asked the driver, who had already taken off his white gloves.
>
> "The devil take it," said Eugène to himself, "since I've started, I must at least get value for my money: 'Drive to the Hôtel de Beauséant,'" he added aloud.
>
> "Which one?" said the driver.
>
> This lofty question shook Eugène's composure. The unfledged dandy was not aware that there were two Hôtels de Beauséant; he did not know how rich he was in relations who did not care a whit about him.
>
> "The vicomte de Beauséant, rue—"
>
> "De Grenelle," interrupted the driver, nodding his head. "You see," he added as he pulled up the step, "There's the count's house and the marquis's in the rue Saint-Dominique."
>
> "Yes, of course," replied Eugène dryly. "Must everyone jeer at me today?" (3:103)

Even to move about Paris in a cab requires some knowledge of how the city is symbolically and physically laid out, and in the absence of such knowledge one risks looking like a fool. Rastignac's ignorance is immediately exposed. At this point, he decides to throw himself on the mercy of the only one who can begin to show him where the bridges between the parts of the city can be found, Mme. de Beauséant herself. It is interesting to note that his transition into her domestic space at the end of his cab ride is every bit as clumsy as his entry into the Restaud household only minutes earlier: "As Eugène was getting out of the cab he heard smothered laughter from under the peristyle. Three or four lackeys had been cracking jokes at the expense of this vulgar bridal equipage. A moment later the student knew in a flash what they were making merry over, as he compared his carriage with one of the most elegant carriages in Paris" (3:104). Little has been changed by Rastignac's extravagant, impulsive decision to take a cab. The comparison between the cab and the elegant carriage parked in the courtyard of the Hôtel de Beauséant is enough to elicit the mirth of the servants once again, because to arrive in a cab is hardly better socially than to arrive on foot. Although Rastignac makes exactly the same mistakes he made previously, this time he is saved by the fact that he is Mme. de Beauséant's cousin. For that reason alone she does not throw him out on his ear. Instead he receives a detailed geography lesson from her and discovers the relation between old Goriot's space and that of his daughters—as well as the difference between the Faubourg Saint-Germain and the Faubourg Saint-Honoré.

Michel de Certeau argues that city architects and urban planners apply conceptions to urban space that the users themselves modify profoundly every day in completely unexpected ways.[20] This is in part Rastignac's project: to become a user of Parisian city space with all the independence that this might imply. I have suggested, in fact, that strategies of communication in densely populated cities such as Paris require a detailed exploration of complex intersections. Limits and boundaries are so compressed that unexpected convergences quickly become the rule rather than the exception. The speed that was at the heart of my earlier analysis of movement on roads across longer distances now becomes the instantaneous, electrical discharge of surprise contained in the encounters provoked by vicinities. And the passages creating these vicinities become crucial objects of knowledge. The density of the network of Parisian passages thus requires a different strategy of communication, one which is symptomatically represented by the act of walking. Not surprisingly, the *flâneur,* the ever present character of mid-nineteenth-century narratives about Paris, takes the place of the walker of previous generations, whose peregrinations between towns and cities were characterized by meditation and an extended communion with nature. The encounters that befall the *flâneur,* on the contrary, are shocks, the electrical shocks so prized by Baudelaire and theorized a century later by Walter Benjamin.

3 *Performances: Horses, Optical Telegraphs (Stendhal)*

In the first part of Stendhal's novel *Lucien Leuwen,* when the principal female character, Mme. de Chasteller, begins to fall in love with the male protagonist, Lucien Leuwen, she tries desperately to understand who he really is and what he might be worth, both from a moral and from a social perspective. One of her greatest fears is expressed in the following manner: "Perhaps he's simply a cavalry officer, like all the others."[1] Mme. de Chasteller wants to know whether Lucien is nothing more than a man adept at riding and maneuvering a powerful horse, or whether there is considerably more to his character (which is, of course, what she hopes). Her first reaction to him is almost inevitable in the narrative logic of the novel, because whatever other personal qualities and distinctive attributes Lucien possesses, one thing is certain and is a given from the start: he is at the very least quite *un homme de cheval,* quite an expert horseman. In his inimitable way, Stendhal will go about demonstrating this in a series of comical sketches that are something like the exceptions that prove the rule. Lucien Leuwen is justly famous for his falls and near falls from his horse—more often than not right beneath Mme. de Chasteller's window and thus in full view of the very woman he wants to impress with his dexterity as a rider. But, of course, that is the point: she wants to see more in him than his riding skills, and his failures fuel her desire. In any case, as early as the first description of Lucien in the novel, while he is still in Paris and well before the scene of the first fall in Nancy, the narrator makes horsemanship a crucial element in the presentation of his protagonist: "In fact, he was rather tall and was a perfectly trained rider" (1:170). Later, as we shall see, his entry into Nancy and the first hours he spends there are filled with incidents and comments regarding his prowess on a horse.

Assuredly, there is something profoundly biographical here. Stendhal's readers know that the novelist was an experienced rider, if not the elegant horseman that he paints in the person of Lucien Leuwen. It is worthwhile recalling that with the help of his cousin, Pierre Daru, Stendhal became a cavalry officer and served in Napoleon's armies from 1800 to 1802. After resigning his commission, he was reintegrated in 1806 into what we would call today the quartermaster general's office, the section of the army in charge of getting men, equipment, and supplies to the right place in the timeliest manner. As a result of his military experiences, Stendhal knew intimately what it took to travel on the system of roads that existed in France during the Napoleonic period and afterwards. He observed at close range the exigencies of the emperor, who wanted troops and supplies to move quickly and expeditiously. Among other highlights of Stendhal's military career of travel through various Napoleonic theaters of war, his difficult trip back from Russia on clogged roads—some of which were barely passable—after the defeat of the imperial army was certainly an experience that marked him. Among many memorable moments in Stendhal's autobiographical texts recounting trips on horseback, moreover, *La Vie de Henri Brulard* ends with a description of the difficult passage through the Saint-Bernard pass across the mountains into Italy: "My horse seemed like it was going to fall, the captain was swearing and filled with gloom. . . . I was soaked, we were constantly encountering obstacles" (377).

Fittingly, then, *Lucien Leuwen* opens with a story of troops on the move, albeit not during the Napoleonic wars but rather during the Restoration. After the political problems that led to Lucien's expulsion from the École Polytechnique are briefly described in the novel's incipit, followed by Lucien's incapacity to decide what might be a possible career in a post-heroic (meaning postimperial) Restoration society, the narrator outlines Lucien's father's solution to the dilemma. He purchases for his son a charge as a second lieutenant in a cavalry regiment to be stationed in Nancy. The regiment sets out for Nancy before Lucien can complete his preparations for departure, and he therefore has to ride in a coach with his immediate superior, Lieutenant Colonel Filloteau, in order to catch up with the troops and join the march. When Filloteau and Lucien finally reach their unit en route toward Nancy, a horse is assigned to Lucien, and he subsequently accompanies his fellow officers during the remainder of the march. The horse is immediately problematic, a sorry excuse for a mount, actually, which nearly throws Stendhal's hero at one point during the march even before he arrives in Nancy. A little later, when the troops finally enter Nancy, the horse will cause Lucien's most embarrassing moment in the town—his fall precisely in front of the window from which Mme. de Chasteller is watching the parade: "Lucien, whose eyes were transfixed on the parrot-green window, spurred on his horse, which slipped and fell, throwing him to the ground. To get up, to strike the nag with the sheath of his sword, to jump back in the saddle took only an instant, in truth, but the laughter was loud and shared by all. Lucien noticed that the woman . . . was still smiling once he had already remounted" (1:794).

I have written in some detail about the theoretical implications of this fall and the one that follows it later in the novel from the point of view of the question of chance, but let us concentrate here more particularly on the immediate results of the incident.[2] Because of his embarrassment following the disastrous fall, the first thing Lucien does when he arrives at his barracks in Nancy is to go directly to the *maître de poste,* Bouchard, to inquire whether in all of Nancy there might be a suitable horse for sale. As *maître de poste,* Bouchard is the logical person to whom Lucien should turn. He undoubtedly owns the most horses of anyone in town, and in his professional capacity he should be the most knowledgeable person concerning the quality of the region's horses in general. In the course of the conversation, Bouchard first tries to make fun of Lucien, who will have nothing of it, whereupon the *maître de poste* informs him that the sub-prefect of the district, Fléron, owns an English thoroughbred: "If you know how to ride, M. Fléron, our prefect, has just what you need: an English thoroughbred sold to him by an English lord who lives around here. The horse is well known to *amateurs:* a superb hock, admirable shoulders, worth three thousand francs, and it has only thrown M. Fléron four times—for the simple reason that the prefect has dared ride it only four times" (1:796). The conversation starts ironically, provided we keep in mind that Lucien's initial fall is precisely what brings him to Bouchard in the first place. The *maître de poste* anticipates a spectacle, believing that Lucien will be thrown again, this time from a horse that has bested the sub-prefect every time that unhappy government official has attempted to mount it. Bouchard prepares to mock Lucien and challenges him with a carefully worded prelude: "If you know how to ride." To add difficulty to the situation, Lara, the horse, has not been exercised properly (no one dares try) and is skittish at best when she is brought out to Lucien: "Lucien had great difficulty mounting and then controlling the horse" (1:799). He succeeds, nonetheless, and rides away at a gallop, returning only after a good half hour—with no mud on his uniform, which Bouchard carefully inspects: "As for the *maître de poste,* he was really hoping to see the horse come back alone. Seeing that it was returning with the rider, he carefully examined Lucien's uniform—nothing indicated that there had been a fall" (1:799). Lucien proceeds to buy the horse outright.

Beneath the surface of this amusing narrative sequence (as only Stendhal can compose them) lies a serious debate about which horses are best for which purposes and which style of riding should be adopted for each type of horse. The English thoroughbred and the style of riding necessary to master such horses were introduced into France only around the middle of the eighteenth century, as one of the results of a general French Anglomania during that period. "The eccentricity of the gallop, a natural gait, of course, but nonetheless violent, ultimate, exorbitant, was not imported from across the Channel until the Anglomania of the nobility in the middle of the eighteenth century. The English thoroughbred flies [*file ventre à terre*] from one point to another in an abstract movement, linear, like an arrow, in harmony with the British taste for betting and for extreme speed between two [racetrack] poles," as Christophe Studeny has argued (58). This description points to several crucial elements. Thoroughbred horses were known for their exaggerated linear, horizontal movement at maximum speed: linear because abrupt maneuvering at full gallop was not possible, horizontal because the combination of horse and rider had to adopt a much less upright position in order to create maximum velocity. Studeny's description points to this when he adopts a traditional French expression to describe the fleet gait of the speeding horse, which moves *ventre à terre.* The trajectory of a horse attaining its full speed is "abstract," almost surreal. It defies the natural obstacles of the terrain, smoothing out its accidents and rough spots, turning it into the equivalent of the flattened surface of a race track.

To master this almost unnatural velocity requires a different riding style, one that was little known in France, frowned upon, in fact, and often refused outright when the first thoroughbreds appeared in French circles. French riding style called for a more upright position, poorly adapted to the performance of a thoroughbred: "French riders, used to an upright style, a dignified bearing, refused this horizontal racing, this debauchery of energy" (59). At the very least, such a horse required unpracticed skills and habits that were foreign to the repertoires of French riders of the period. These issues were the subject of a military debate about speed and about the best horses necessary to accomplish the most favorable results in military campaigns. Not unexpectedly, Napoleon weighed in with his own strong opinion on these questions. Studeny's discussion underscores this: "It was all well and good for Napoleon to declare, 'Extreme speed doesn't make a good horse for the purposes of war; it takes pliancy, dexterity, intelligence, docility.' The thoroughbred, reputedly fragile, defied his soldiers. The English would send single officers on racehorses to observe the maneuvers of the enemy. . . . The French would give chase, but in vain. The [English] scouts would turn tail and run, to the despair of the French generals" (59). Quite unexpectedly for French military strategists of the period, pure speed did create a military advantage.

Echoes of this controversy appear in the text of *Lucien Leuwen* at two different moments. The first occurs during a formal ceremony welcoming Lucien to the regiment. As Colonel Mahler's horse approaches Lucien's, the colonel's horse makes an unexpected movement in the wrong direction, and Lucien responds by maneuvering Lara in a way that covers the colonel's mistake without the slightest visible effort to guide his horse—almost as if the horse had accomplished the adjustment naturally. Leuwen gains the admiration of the regiment's officers, both for his maneuver and for Lara's willingness to obey him: "And people say that English thoroughbreds are unmanageable! . . . They are unmanageable for those who do not know how to manage them" (1:814). The commentator, one of the soldiers in attendance, implies that criticisms made concerning the qualities of the English thoroughbred are really criticisms of riders who do not know the proper technique for controlling this particular breed of horses. The second evidence of the debate about riding styles can be found in chapter 31 of the first part of the novel. This chapter is curiously interjected into the middle of a scene that takes place in Mme. d'Hocquincourt's salon.[3] The narrator interrupts his description of the scene to speak about another thoroughbred, Soliman, owned by Lord Link, the very person who sold Lara to the sub-prefect Fléron in the first place, and therefore the original owner of Lucien's present horse.[4] Lucien has seen horse and rider on the roads around Nancy and describes Soliman as follows: "The horse doesn't seem to touch the ground or rather it seems that the ground is elastic and that it projects him into the air when he is moving in lively fashion, for example, when he is trotting" (1:1021). This description of the horse's motion corresponds closely to the horizontal projection underlined by Studeny and to the "abstract" nature of the magnificent animal's movement through space. It is as if, Lucien intones, the horse were suspended in midair. And when it does touch the ground, the surface seems to add even more spring to the energy it generates. The riding style of the horse's owner, moreover, calls immediate attention to the differences French riders perceived between their own style and that of English riders: "The rider was skilled, but his demeanor was that of a stable boy who had just won first prize in the Viennese lottery" (1:1020). Lucien is willing to recognize the strength and skill necessary to control such a horse, but he criticizes the style even more pointedly several paragraphs later: "[He] rode quite well, but with too much arm movement" (1:1021). This is an explicit remark on the perceived differences of riding styles between the English and the French. As we saw, French riders preferred a dignified demeanor that minimized bodily movement, whereas the English did not hesitate to espouse the horizontal motion of the horse with their own bodies. Although Lucien is the critic here and seems to pit himself against the Englishman, the fact remains that he knows enough about the English riding technique to be able to apply it to his own mastery of Lara. Otherwise, he would have found himself quickly thrown to the ground like the sub-prefect, who is unable to control the skittish and powerful thoroughbred because he is unable to adjust his body posture correctly.

The performances of English thoroughbreds, then, were possible only if equaled in physical prowess by those of their riders. One must not forget that to gallop at sustained speeds is a demanding physical exercise: "The sustained gallop is like a physical test in the exhausting relation between muscular power of the horse and the endurance of the rider, combined with the resistance of the ground" (Studeny 56). Three factors had to coincide to realize the full potential for velocity: horse, rider, and terrain. French military thinkers had suggested that taken out of its milieu, the flattened surface of a racetrack, the thoroughbred would be of little use in wartime. The experience of the imperial wars showed otherwise. The pace of the thoroughbred represented the maximum attainable velocity on the speed scale of overland transportation at the time. English scouts had a decided advantage when spying on French lines, because French horses and riding styles did not permit French cavalry officers to catch English riders mounted on this new type of horse.[5] Lucien's association with English horses and riding habits in *Lucien Leuwen* is no accident. Stendhal purposely situates his protagonist in the category of those who know how to mobilize the most advanced technologies of speed associated with the horse.

The term "technology" is used here in a way that might seem unexpected, but when one begins to reflect on the notion of speed before the invention and development of the steam engine and the railroad, one quickly realizes that the use of the horse as a means of transportation had long before created a new situation in which the velocity attainable by a rider—at least for short bursts—far exceeded the capacities of the human body. At stake is clearly a technology. Paul Virilio takes this view in a discussion in *L'Horizon négatif* dealing with the use of the horse in ancient civilizations: "The horse is thus indispensable to the assumption of the passenger, who is a rider levitated above the ground, a hostage of velocity, deprived of his own motivity. . . . The horse's saddle is related to a piece of furniture, a hippomobile seat that would not only assist the body in the practice of immobility, of remaining still, as in the case of a chair, but also in the exercise of movement from one place to the other"[6] (41). The horse saddled and mounted, as Virilio describes it, already possesses the characteristics of our ultramodern vehicles that go hundreds of times faster. In order to use the horse, the rider must be immobilized upon the animal's back, so that the power of locomotion is entirely given over to the animal. This strange combination of immobility and mobility is not completely unlike that of the astronaut strapped in a seat in the nose cone of a rocket, although, admittedly, on a radically different scale.

To attain the velocities possible with English horses required a substantially different type of physical performance on the part of the rider. Lucien's success is directly related to his skill at assuming the correct posture permitting the immobility necessary to be projected horizontally at high speed. This demands an uncommon amount of physical strength and manual dexterity, a panoply of talents that Lucien must demonstrate to all the nobles in Nancy, precisely because they know about his fall in the rue de la Pompe, the incident that makes him an inevitable topic of conversation. He atones for his riding error by his *hardiesse,* his daring, a term that recurs with some frequency in descriptions of his style on horseback: "The slightly pretentious daring with which he maneuvered the prefect's well-known and quite dangerous horse . . . had made him a considerable personage for many people [in Nancy]" (1:808). Mme. de Chasteller echoes this theme: "At least this young officer was not timid on a horse. He made her tremble every day by his daring, and a daring so often unlucky, she added almost laughing" (1:920). It is fitting, then, that the end of the first part of *Lucien Leuwen,* when Lucien flees to Paris, takes the form of a performance in horsemanship that requires prodigious physical stamina: Leuwen returns to Paris from Nancy on horseback in around thirty-two hours (1:1064). The minimal distance between the two cities by road during the 1830s can be estimated at about 320 kilometers, and the calculation is therefore simple: 10 kilometers an hour means that Lucien's average speed was equivalent to a sustained trot for the entire trip. More accurately, the trip was probably composed of bursts of galloping in combination with moments of less rapid motion. One must factor into this equation the time needed to change post horses, which makes the performance all the more impressive. It would be fair to say that Lucien's trip is made in outstanding time—it is hard to imagine a better performance for a rider under the overland travel conditions of the historical period in question.

Lucien's performance can only underline more clearly, moreover, the connection between the "technology" of the horse and that of the development of the road network. As Virilio reminds us: "The first 'military clearing,' the road is simply a linear deciphering offered to the 'divine celerity' of the tank, an earth scorched by vehicles, a scoured surface. . . . *Speed creates a vacuum, a vacuum creates speed*" (*L'Horizon négatif* 49, Virilio's italics). The space in between departure point and destination point is a space that has been maximally emptied of obstacles in order to provide for the rider's best performance. It was precisely during the fifty years before the setting of *Lucien Leuwen* that major strides were made in France in the building and upkeep of roads. In abstract terms, the road is a man-made attempt to empty the infinitely varied topography of the terrains one might encounter, to make that topography utterly uniform and thus susceptible to the performances of vehicles. What Lucien tests with his own performance at the close of the first part of Stendhal's novel is something like the state of the road system and the organization of the post relays at the beginning of the decade of the 1830s. Ultimately, the thoroughbred at the thematic heart of the first part of the novel is precisely that technological machine capable of turning nearly any terrain into a racetrack.

In my analysis of Balzac's *Un Début dans la vie,* the imbrication of the movement of people and of messages was stressed, because the two are linked in fascinating ways into a broader communicational system. This is certainly the case in *Lucien Leuwen* as well, because if Lucien's expertise as a horseman well versed in the technologies of velocity is a principal theme of the first part of the novel, his familiarity with the use and abuse of the optical telegraph system in the second half of the novel is a logical outgrowth of that expertise. Lucien's talents as a rider of the fastest breed of horses of his day are a prelude to his expert manipulation of the period's fastest messaging system. When Leuwen leaves Nancy and returns to Paris, he takes a position as personal secretary to the Minister of the Interior, the principal administrator controlling the telegraph. Until the postal reform begun in 1873 and completed only in 1878, which reorganized the bureaucratic structure of the postal system in France, the French telegraph network (first optical and then electrical) remained—for strategic reasons—under the control of the Ministry of the Interior and was not a part of the postal system. The French government, through all its phases for over a century—republic, empire, monarchy, or constitutional monarchy—invariably refused to merge the telegraph system with the post office until ultimately the government of the Third Republic broke the logjam and restructured what had become an unjustifiable double administration. The split between the two message services—post office and telegraph—was not arbitrary. It reflected a calculated executive decision affecting strategic policy. Telegraphic communication was considered too important for national politics and international diplomacy (the one obviously closely related to the other) to leave it open and in the public domain.

Hints of Lucien's association with various kinds of messages and with the media used to convey them already appear in the first part of the novel. While he is in Paris, before the military enlistment that sends him to Nancy, for example, his father has him work in the family business once a week, on Thursdays, "jour du grand courrier de Hollande," the day of the week when correspondence from Holland necessary for the banking business arrives in the mail (Leuwen's father's bank is associated with a Dutch bank). Even before Lucien realizes that his father's bank engages in speculation based on optical telegraph information, the nobles in Nancy have verified his social standing by obtaining knowledge about his father's activities, and they therefore know that this type of risky investment strategy is characteristic of Van Peters, Leuwen, and Company: "This bank . . . is among the few that occasionally buy news from ministers, or that exploit the news and share with them the profits thus generated" (1:893). Such carefully gathered intelligence allows Lucien's rivals in Nancy to know whom they are confronting, but the issues raised here actually prefigure the novel's ending. As the narrator comments pointedly, "this bad sort of business . . . brings ultimate ruin, but . . . makes for agreeable and well-placed relations" (1:893). A bankruptcy doubtless provoked by a series of speculative ventures of the telegraphic sort puts an end to Lucien's father's bank in the final pages of the second part of the novel.[7] During Lucien's stay in Nancy in the novel's first part, then, others know a good deal more about his father's uses of the telegraph than Lucien can yet imagine.

When Lucien starts to work for the Minister of the Interior, however, things change dramatically, and his connection to telegraph messaging becomes much more direct and evident. One could even claim that this is one of the central issues of the second part of the novel. A projected but abandoned title of the story was, fittingly, *Le Télégraphe.* Before we turn to a detailed analysis of the presence of this technological innovation in *Lucien Leuwen,* a brief description of the telegraph system that has such important effects on the story must be provided. It is easy to pass rapidly over the mention of the telegraph in the novel and thereby to miss much of the complex technological/political revolution that it represented. What Stendhal is talking about is the optical or semaphore telegraph conceived and built by the Chappe brothers beginning in 1792. An electrified network began to be installed extensively in France only at the very end of the 1840s and the beginning of the 1850s. Between 1792, when the optical telegraph system began to be developed, and 1852, when it was finally taken out of service because the installation of an electrical telegraph network had reached a point where it offered a more dependable, flexible, and economically feasible service than the *télégraphe aérien,* as Chappe had baptized it, the optical telegraph network grew to the point where it "comprised nineteen branches, and a total length of more than 4000 kilometers, including 556 stations."[8] The routes followed by this extensive network radiated out from Paris in a starlike shape, mimicking what would later be the layout of the major railroad lines in France and what had already been the main organizational layout of the royal roads.

Materially speaking, the optical telegraph consisted of a series of stations (relays) on the top of which were installed windmill-like arms. The stations were ideally situated on hills or promontories (often in disaffected church towers) in order to make them visible from greater distances. Messages were transmitted using a table of codes, associated with the positions of the arms of the machine, to the next station visible by telescope down or up the line from the first. Without entering into too much detail concerning the structure of this message-sending apparatus, suffice it to say that a long arm, attached to a pole at its center, could be pivoted 180 degrees around its center pin. At each extremity of the arm, an additional smaller pivoting arm was fixed. Each of the three arms was capable of assuming a variety of angles, and the various discrete positions formed by the combinations of the positions of the three arms could be assigned meaning. The apparatus of the arms was controlled by a system of pulleys running from the arms down to control levers inside the station that were manipulated by the operator. In fact, the levers allowed the operator to pass signals along by simple rote repetition of the arm positions, because the levers mimicked the positions of the arms on top of the telegraph tower. Stations were generally six to eight miles apart, that is, the maximum distance at which an operator with a telescope could distinguish clearly the positions relayed by the next station up the line. Messages were sent only during daylight hours and under acceptable weather conditions. Fog and rain interfered with transmissions, and although there was originally hope to construct semaphore mechanisms visible at night, no successful system for night transmissions was ever devised.

So much for the basic structure of the telegraph stations in the network. It would be useful as well to give some indications about the conditions of its invention and eventual construction on so large a scale. As Patrice Carré has reminded us in a short paper on the origin of the optical telegraph in France, the network was born at a time of revolutionary crisis when France was threatened by powerful European monarchs, who did not want to see the French Revolution succeed.[9] Prominent members of a whole scientific and engineering generation were favorable to the republic and used their talents to defend in various ways the successes of the Revolution (Monge, Fourier, Chaptal, Berthollet, and Carnot are a few examples among many others). It was in the context of the great dangers of 1791 and 1792 that Claude Chappe first proposed the construction of a semaphore telegraph network that could improve communication and allow the republic to react quickly to international threats, but also to coordinate its own internal operations. Chappe and his brothers persuaded the legislative assembly to fund experiments aimed at proving that high-speed communication was possible and that it could be of great use to the republic. The experiments led to the construction of the first lengthy line of the network, namely, Paris-Lille: "The line, 210 km. in length, appears to have operated regularly from the end of Thermidor, An II (mid-August 1794). Although correspondence between Claude and Abraham Chappe deplored hitches in transmission the new medium was soon working well enough to announce news which dispelled doubts of its value" (Wilson 123).

These basic historical facts underscore the link between a revolutionary politico-military complex and the invention and propagation of the optical telegraph network in France. The network did not spring up as a pure engineering feat but as an emblematic artifact created at the conjunction between the technological and the social. In fact, the notion of a truly elaborated semaphore messaging system had been discussed in various forms for nearly a century. When the system finally began to be built, it was not the result of a new technological invention but, rather, the development of an already existing technology that was given an extensive material form because of a specific political situation. As Patrice Flichy has argued cogently, moreover, the military dangers confronting the new French republic were not the only motivating factors. The revolutionary government had undertaken a rethinking of the whole organization of French national space and time, as indicated by the attempt to enforce the use of a new calendar, a new system of measurement (the metric system), and a national language that would be the same for all French citizens (8–15). This complex origin goes a long way toward explaining the system's constant link thereafter to the political security apparatus of the French government and ultimately to the principal bureaucracy charged with maintaining that security, the Ministry of the Interior, described in *Lucien Leuwen* in its incarnation under the July Monarchy. It is interesting to note that three Chappe brothers, Abraham, Ignace, and Pierre-François, who continued constructing and administering the telegraph system under Napoleon after Claude Chappe's untimely suicide, survived the purge of administrators after Napoleon's fall and retained their positions in the telegraph administration during the first years of the Restoration (Wilson 137). Agnostic with respect to the type of regime in place, the telegraph was nonetheless decidedly not agnostic with respect to the state—it was clearly an arm of state government. The Chappe brothers were emblematic members of a state bureaucracy intent on running the mechanisms of governance without regard to political parties. Whether it was the imperial regime or the Restoration, the telegraph administrators knew state secrets before anyone else but generally kept them from both the public and the opposition, thereby cultivating a code of neutrality that would be the envy of any contemporary French "énarque."[10]

An important means of communication for state affairs, the optical telegraph was thus a monopoly jealously guarded by the various regimes between 1792 and 1852 and kept out of the public domain. The Chappe family and others repeatedly proposed schemes to commercialize the telegraph system and to allow it to be leveraged to make money. Using it to transmit news for printing in regional newspapers or for transmitting stock market quotations were two suggestions that recurred with some regularity. The only use other than military or diplomatic that Napoleon permitted was the broadcasting of winning lottery numbers, in order to prevent the fraud that was possible in the delay between the drawings in Paris and the announcement of the winning numbers in provincial towns (any delay raised the specter of the printing of counterfeit tickets containing the winning numbers and cashed in before the officially printed winning tickets could be presented in regional lottery offices). But this should not give us even a moment's pause in our understanding of the state monopoly of the telegraph network: the lottery was organized and controlled by the state and was thus simply another governmental function using a means of communication reserved for governmental purposes.

Lucien Leuwen is destined to encounter telegraph messaging almost from the beginning of his career in the office of the Minister of the Interior. In the first place, the telegraph is at the center of an ethical reflection about whether Lucien can do what it takes to work for a minister under the conditions of the Restoration. His father's question is simple: "To what extent do you feel strong enough to be a rogue, that is, to engage in roguish activities?" (1:1073). Lucien does not immediately realize that this question points implicitly to the telegraph speculations that his minister will undertake. The lesson is not long in coming, however. Several days after he begins working as the secretary to the interior minister, M. de Vaize, the minister comes running into his office obviously disturbed by something: "Run to your father. . . . But first copy this telegraph message" (1:1106). It takes Lucien only a few moments of reflection to realize what is at stake here: "His Excellency is most certainly playing the stock market. . . . And here I am clearly the accomplice in this knavery" (1:1107). A question is thus immediately raised about the relation between the official use of the telegraph and its unofficial, if not to say fraudulent, use. The same news that is essential for running the affairs of state is also essential for getting a head start on other investors and taking positions in the stock market before anyone else, thereby maximizing profits by initiating trends rather than following them after they have begun. In some sense, one could say that the problem of "insider" information is endemic to stock market speculation and that the existence of the telegraph exacerbates the situation. Powerful banks in European countries already had private mail services well before the construction of semaphore telegraph systems, services that allowed them to get information before anyone else—including governments—and subsequently to manipulate markets in ways unavailable to private citizens and to governments alike. With the telegraph in France under the Restoration, the office of the Minister of the Interior becomes, among other things, a hotbed of insider information. In any case, as we moderns know very well, the limit beyond which insider information becomes fraudulent and manipulative is notoriously hard to locate. And Lucien's father quickly explains that the ascent of M. de Vaize to the position of Minister of the Interior is directly linked to speculation on telegraph news: "I made his ministry a success, I was behind his nomination to the stock exchange, and for a percentage, I agreed to take care of all dealings based on telegraph messages" (1:1114). The implications could not be clearer: the minister owes his credibility to a campaign orchestrated by the bankers, one of whom, in return, is a regular conduit for investment news delivered by the minister hot off the telegraph tower.

The development of the optical telegraph network in France and its unavailability to any but a select few (the governmental bureaucracy and banking allies) turns out to be a key issue in a long debate about the democratization of information, a debate that was particularly marked by the development of the newspaper during the same period. An emblematic perspective on this debate can be found a little later in Louis Blanc's *Lettres sur l'Angleterre,* Deuxième Série, written while he was in exile in England in 1863, and published in 1866. Blanc analyzes the development of the English newspaper, the *Times,* which already early in the nineteenth century had become a powerful public source of information that escaped government control and worked against the exclusive access to news that governments (and bankers) were attempting to protect. Writes Blanc referring to the company that had invented the *Times* and turned it into the informational tool that it later became:

> An extraordinary spirit of enterprise was demonstrated in the efforts undertaken by the company to gather news, and during the wars that followed the French Revolution, it found a way to receive from the continent messages that came faster than those sent by the government. In other countries, the spectacle of a government thus beaten by a private enterprise would have seemed scandalous. But the idea that for a modest sum and without even going out of their own homes, people could know as much as a minister pleased the English, and they rejoiced in the success of the company in its struggle against the government. From that moment onward, the power of the newspaper grew to the point where it became the top newspaper in the world. (1:2–3)

The policy debate about whether to make the optical telegraph a state monopoly or a private commercial venture (that is, whether to maintain governmental control of the medium or to allow public access to it and to the news it purveyed) came to a head in France in 1837, when a law was promulgated establishing a prison sentence for "whosoever transmits, without authorization, signals from one place to another" (Flichy 22–23). Flichy summarizes succinctly the terms of the debate that led to the passage of this law (22–24). In a first stage, during discussions that preceded the vote on the law in question, many legislators expressed a disdain for the crass commercialism of the growing French bourgeoisie. They saw the privatization and commercialization of the telegraph system as a means that threatened to extend the unethical speculative practices of a predatory commercial class victimizing the rest of French society: "The deputy Fulchiron could thus declare: 'Until now I have never seen telegraphic lines established by a private person with good intentions'; they serve to 'establish a brigandage, so as to rob those who do not have news of the Paris Bourse'" (Flichy 23). Moreover, France had just experienced a period of political unrest, and a real fear existed that a privatized telegraph system could be used to organize oppositional forces and mobilize them against the monarchy.

As Flichy suggests, however, immediate fears and dislikes of this sort are a poor basis for a sweeping legislative project reaffirming a strong and exclusive state monopoly on the telegraph system, and the debate was ultimately transformed into a wider and more principled discussion about democratic access to information. A comparison between the post office and the telegraph immediately arose. If the post office, run by the state, allowed private citizens access to its services, why should the telegraph system not do the same? A complex and fascinating position of principle emerged:

> The argument ran as follows: the mail could transport a considerable number of dispatches all arriving at the same time, so that it was difficult to manipulate information. A letter could be contradicted by another one which arrived at the same time. "But the telegraph does not lend itself to such freedom, that equality, that simultaneous action. In itself it excludes such competition and the telegraph is, necessarily, a monopoly. . . ." The monopolistic aspect of the telegraph was due mainly to the conditions of transmission. Potential traffic on a line was limited and nothing guaranteed that a dispatch sent half an hour or an hour after another one would arrive the same day. "Will not the first one enjoy an immense, exorbitant, inadmissible privilege?" (23–24)

The optical telegraph system of the period provided no economically feasible means for solving the bottleneck of communication created by single telegraph communication lines, available, moreover, only during daylight and under good weather conditions. Those lines had not proliferated into a veritable network, with transverse connections and thus multiple trajectories possible for messages sent, because to build such interconnections required major investments (property purchases, architectural construction of the towers, numerous employees to maintain additional stations). Only with the advent of the electrical telegraph, with its considerably lighter infrastructure investment demands (the difference between constructing towers and stringing electrical lines from pole to pole) could a system that avoided the bottleneck described above be envisaged. We shall return to the notion of information overload and its consequences when we read Alexandre Dumas's novel *Le Comte de Monte-Cristo,* but those consequences are already clearly envisaged in the terms of the parliamentary debate about the status of the telegraph system. In the absence of an access to messaging that would allow competing perspectives on events to confront one another synchronically, it is simply too easy to manipulate the news. Since bad weather or the setting of the sun could end transmissions for a considerable number of hours, news transmitted by one correspondent could gain an unjust advantage in the absence of any competing perspectives that might allow those who received the message to judge its validity more objectively.

Lucien Leuwen's first experience with the telegraph in the Ministry of the Interior immediately raises the ethical question of "parasiting" the system in the sense Michel Serres gives to that term. In *The Parasite,* Serres argues that every communicational system is cascading, that is, the channel between two relay points that carries messages or goods can always be tapped into at the next level by a third party of some form or another (3–25). The telegraph system is designed to carry politico-military news to facilitate centralized state decisions, but those who have access to it invariably turn it toward other ends. This fraud is at the heart of the political system that Lucien encounters when he goes to work for M. de Vaize in the Ministry of the Interior, as we saw earlier. We shall return to the question of fraud shortly in the context of *Le Comte de Monte-Cristo,* but it is important to underline the second characteristic of the telegraph system suggested by the short scene with which we began, the one during which de Vaize instructs Lucien to take information to his father: "Run to your father," he says. The operative notion here is *running:* do not simply take this information to M. Leuwen, the minister insists, take it there quickly. The second element foregrounded, then, is speed. The rapidity with which information reaches M. de Vaize is mirrored by the rapidity with which he sends Lucien off to meet M. Leuwen *père.* The information in the telegraph message arrives almost instantaneously, and instantaneity also characterizes the way the information must be dealt with once it is known. Why is this? Being the first to know what de Vaize has discovered will allow him as possessor of such information to make favorable stock purchases, but the moment of opportunity is very short. The distance the information has traveled, great as it might have been from a purely geographical point of view, has been transformed by the telegraphic message into nothing but a small crease in space. Time and space have been compressed to such an extent that a single second lost in the operation will prevent any profit-taking. Lucien, previously the cavalry officer and expert horseman, is now the rapid courier.

One must also note the way in which public and private spaces and times are inextricably woven together here. M. de Vaize is co-opting information crucial to the conduct of French affairs of state and turning it simultaneously to his own private advantage. If indeed time and space are compressed by the telegraph message, the public and the private are also conflated—the space that separates them is negated in the blink of an eye. One could almost say that the increased rhythm of decision making provoked by the use of the telegraph prevents the agents involved from taking any objective distance from the process and assessing how to separate the public from the private. De Vaize has no time to evaluate the fundamental meaning of any aspect of the situation other than the immediate effect of a piece of news on market trends: he must act instantly, without delay. The absence of any objective distance from which one might gain some perspective on one's actions turns de Vaize into little more than a predatory speculator. He becomes a parasite who has succeeded in inserting himself into a circuit of information exchange that was destined for another use and in turning it into a financial bonanza that has nothing to do with the productivity and development of the French economy as a whole. Moreover, and perhaps this is the most fascinating issue here, the intensive speed-related speculation allowed by insider telegraph information quickly begins to blur the distinctions between cause and effect. The logical assumption would be that certain news items cause the market to fluctuate, but as the speed with which information is exchanged over the telegraph lines increases, a legitimate question begins to arise: Is it actually the news that produces a given market trend or is it the positions taken by speculators in the know, who, because they take a certain position, can virtually cause the very market movement upon which they are betting? The asymptotic near-coincidence between the event and the reporting of the event, about which Jean Baudrillard has had much to say in recent years and about which Virilio also writes often, is already contained in larval form in M. de Vaize's behavior.

The second use of the telegraph—explored in even greater detail in the second half of the novel—is its mobilization in an attempt to change the outcome of a provincial electoral campaign. As we have seen from the beginning, politics and speculation are the two principal domains on which the telegraph had an immediate and lasting impact from the beginning of the establishment of the semaphore network in France. Lucien's minister sends him, along with an aide named Coffe, to Caen in order to do all that is possible to prevent the election of an enemy of the monarchy, M. Mairobert. Not surprisingly, one of the first questions that arises, as de Vaize outlines the assignment to Lucien, is access to the telegraph system. Lucien needs to correspond rapidly with M. de Vaize in the Ministry of the Interior in Paris to seek approval for the various strategies he will have to invent in the heat of the moment: "Don't worry," de Vaize reassures him, "You will have the telegraph" (1:1187). Simple access to the telegraph is not enough, however; the conditions of that access are also crucial. Lucien responds: "I plan to act prudently, but ultimately can I correspond by telegraph with Your Excellency without communicating what I am saying to the prefect?" "Yes, you have my consent," the minister replies (1:1188). Control of the space in between sender and receiver demands that intermediaries be removed, that the space between relays be cleared of all obstacles.

Once assured of this direct and exclusive access, Lucien and Coffe begin their trip with a coach ride toward Caen that recalls in familiar detail many of the elements that came up in our analysis of Balzac's *Un Début dans la vie.* In particular, during the coach ride, the connection between mail and passengers is reworked. Lucien and Coffe have been given packages containing copies of a pamphlet, which they are planning to distribute in order to try to undercut the credibility of the antigovernment candidate, Mairobert, once they arrive in Caen. The pamphlet, carried as mail to be delivered to the prefect for distribution by his agents, is in perfect parallel with the passengers' assigned task in the affair, that is, to serve as governmental *agents provocateurs* in the last-minute electoral maneuvering that will take place in Caen. Leuwen and Coffe think they are traveling incognito in the safety of their coach. Unfortunately, however, as they enter Blois, where they are to eat dinner en route, a packet of pamphlets falls off the coach onto the roadway and is discovered by the citizens of Blois, who subsequently threaten to stone the carriage. Lucien and Coffe are forced to flee the town ignominiously (1:1189–91). The crowd makes no distinction between Lucien's person and the crude pamphlets he is carrying in the coach. Lucien might well try to defend his ethics and good intentions in his lamentations to Coffe after the incident, but the crowd instantly conflates the mail and the person of the interior minister's envoy.

Once Leuwen and Coffe arrive in Caen, the centrality of communication, and particularly of telegraphic communication, is affirmed. A direct conflict develops between the prefect, M. de Séranville, and Lucien over control of the telegraph. After Lucien has sized up the situation and realized that it will be nearly impossible to influence the election in the three days remaining before the vote, he summarizes his findings and goes to the telegraph office to send his text: "Lucien went out alone to go over to the office of the prefect and walked up to the telegraph office. He had M. Lamorte, the director of the telegraph, read the authorization from his minister and asked him to send his message immediately. The director was uncomfortable and made excuses. Leuwen, who looked at his watch constantly, feared the fog on this winter day and finally spoke firmly. The clerk insinuated that he would do well to go see the prefect" (1:1230). Lucien's impatience underlines the difficulties associated with the optical telegraph during the period. Because it is winter, the reliability of the system is diminished. Winter fog can descend on the region or on some other region in between Caen and Paris, thereby interfering with and delaying transmission of any message. Each minute of clear weather is precious and must be mobilized if messages are to be exchanged successfully. Forced to ask the permission of the prefect to transmit his telegraph message, Leuwen discovers that de Séranville has closed the telegraph office to any transmissions without his permission. He has, moreover, taken measures to prevent the mail from transiting toward Paris by coach or rider, requiring a special passport with his signature to be displayed by any passenger or postal agent who wishes to cross a nearby bridge. These measures effectively prevent Lucien from taking control of the situation. The confrontation between Lucien and the prefect provoked by conflicting rights and responsibilities crystallizes around the question of information transmission and blossoms into a veritable political crisis. Armed with a personal order from the minister allowing him direct and confidential access to the telegraph, Lucien has no recourse but to threaten to arrest M. de Séranville, who is acting against the direct orders of his own superior. It could not be more evident in the course of this incident that control of the space of communication is tantamount to possessing political power and that the telegraph is at the hub of the information network at stake here. Preventing de Séranville from exercising control over communication in his jurisdiction is equivalent to relieving him of his official duties.

One could easily say, moreover, that the notion of the *dépêche télégraphique,* the telegraph message, becomes a veritable stylistic node in this description of electoral struggles in Caen. The presentation of the events in question is punctuated by no less than four telegraph messages from Lucien to his minister, three of which elicit telegraphic responses from the minister, and several of which are quoted verbatim. One of them does, in fact, become the focal point of a rather amusing commentary on style. As Lucien completes the text of his first message, he hands it to Coffe, who, upon rereading it, proposes a correction: "Coffe approved the message, making him remove three words and replace them with a single word" (1:1230). Lucien's self-indulgent overstatement will have to be replaced by what is strictly, bureaucratically necessary. Even more significantly, the messages themselves become an auto-referential element of the whole episode. Lucien ultimately sends messages referring to his own previous messages: "I would consider it a great good fortune if your telegraph message in response to my message number 2 were to arrive tomorrow, the 17th, before two o'clock" (1:1251), he writes to de Vaize at one point, prompting his minister to acknowledge not only the instantaneous nature of the means of communication employed here but the way it must be used with utmost celerity to influence events at the very last instant. Any request transmitted on the telegraph network is truly one that demands instantaneous response. The minister is not to be outdone by his emissary when reacting to the time compression imposed by the telegraph. His first message to Lucien in Caen finishes with the following remark: "M. Leuwen will answer this instant" (1:1232). A foreboding notion, "this instant," because it points emblematically toward our own contemporary quandary with electronic messages: everyone wants a response "this instant," immediately, without delay, with all attention focused on the present above anything else. The whole structure of the Caen election episode contributes to a feverish atmosphere of instantaneity. Given very little time, Lucien must rush around among the parties confronting one another in the election to try to curb a momentum that has been established over months of campaigning. The task is daunting, and it would be impossible were it not for the telegraph. This network allows Lucien to adapt his strategy rapidly, in the heat of events, and to request and receive clearance from his minister when he has to adjust hastily. Because this means of communication functions so expeditiously, the minister can simultaneously empower Lucien and yet refrain from endowing him with complete freedom of maneuver. One can see here how a well-oiled centralized nation state can simultaneously be represented and yet be immediately present in its fullness anywhere on a territory crisscrossed by ultrarapid means of communication such as the optical telegraph.

The ultimate episode of the drama played out during the Caen election in *Lucien Leuwen* comes on the final day of balloting and confirms crucial elements highlighted by our analysis. It introduces as well and very explicitly another dimension of the optical telegraph, namely, its *cultural visibility* in the landscape of the period. The moving arms of its prominent towers could be seen in the course of message transmitting, and the messages therefore had a curious status, both obvious and hidden (one knows messages are being transmitted, but in the absence of a key to the code, one cannot know what they actually contain). As the election proceeds on the final afternoon of Lucien's activities in Caen, his impatience to receive a reply from M. de Vaize concerning his final strategic request is very apparent: "Every fifteen minutes, Lucien sent

Coffe to look at the telegraph; he was burning to see the answer to his message" (1:1257). Rapid exchange of messages breeds the expectation of quick and timely replies to any message sent down the line, as we have just seen. The telegraph tower is visible from quite a distance—if it were not, the semaphore concept of message encoding would simply not work. Its very visibility means that any observer can perceive when the system is in operation and when it is not. The pivoting of the telegraph tower's arms may well appear to be random to anyone who does not have access to the code book, but the bare fact that the arms are in motion signals nonetheless that a message is in transit.

In the present case, Lucien suspects that if the tower arms are at rest, this could simply mean that the prefect has once again ordered a suspension of all activity at the telegraph tower. Such a suspension is *visible:* it cannot be surreptitious, given the prominence of such towers in the landscape. Says Lucien's ally, General Fari, "The prefect is quite capable of delaying this response. . . . It would be quite in character for him to have sent one of his clerks to the telegraph station four leagues from here, on the other side of the hill, to stop everything" (1:1257). Such an act simply cannot remain secret for long. One need only send an observer to a high enough vantage point to have a view of the next station up the line in order to discover whether a message is actually being transmitted from Paris toward Caen. In their haste to learn the outcome of Lucien's request to M. de Vaize (a request, by the way, that involves paying a substantial bribe to garner additional votes against Mairobert), Lucien and the general send Coffe on horseback to check on the next telegraph station down the line: "The diminutive captain Ménière offered to get on a horse and gallop up the mountain to observe any movement at the second telegraph station, but M. Coffe asked the captain for his horse and went in his place" (1:1257). In order to verify whether or not the prefect has actually suspended telegraph operations in Caen, it suffices to get to higher ground and observe the next station down the line to see if movement can be detected. Time presses in a way that summarizes Lucien's whole experience in Caen—he has an impossible task to accomplish in a lapse of time unheard of before the possibility of telegraph messages: "The clock struck two, two thirty; the telegraph did not stir" (1:1257). The striking of the clock on the hour and on the half hour is fast becoming a reference to a past era, because time lapses are now measured instead in minutes and seconds: "Lucien was burning with impatience" (1:1257). Finally, the telegraph comes to life, Coffe runs back to announce that there is a message, and Lucien is able to carry through his last desperate, if unsuccessful, strategic maneuver. Time flies during this whole sequence at a rhythm unimaginable before the telegraph network existed because of its high-speed performance potential.

In the end, the telegraph message becomes a veritable stylistic fetish in *Lucien Leuwen.* One might recall here that Julien Sorel in *Le Rouge et le noir* has a small number of texts (three, in fact) to which he turns constantly to furnish him models, behavior patterns for a life singularly devoid of models to which he can turn for help to cope with the complex society he wants to conquer. One of those texts is none other than the Napoleonic *Bulletins de la Grande Armée* (Napoleonic campaign reports): "The abhorrence for eating with the servants did not come naturally to Julien. In order to make his way in the world he would have done things much more disagreeable. He drew this particular repugnance from Rousseau's *Confessions.* It was the only book that helped him imagine his place in society. The collection of the *Bulletins de la Grande Armée* and the *Mémorial de Sainte-Hélène* rounded out his Koran. He would have given his life for these three works. He never believed in anything else" (1:235). The central importance of the *Bulletins de la Grande Armée,* not only as a model for behavior but also as a standard for terse, pointed, and tasteful reporting prose, is a favorite rhetorical reference for Stendhal the writer. The lesson carries over into *Lucien Leuwen.* The *Bulletins,* summarizing the events on the battlefield, carried in haste between strategic battle positions by the cavalry officer on the fastest horse (like Lucien Leuwen himself), have now been replaced by the *dépêche télégraphique,* the telegraph message, which has become not only a node in a new kind of political strategy but, even more significantly, a veritable model for communication in a developing modern space of instantaneity.[11] Lucien has been converted to this new context, and his skills have been carried over intact. No longer the red and the black, the military and the clergy, but now the black and the white, the white noise against which significant signals are foregrounded in this new economy of speed that the telegraphic message is creating.

Laurence de Cinq-Cygne, the heroine of Balzac's *Une Ténébreuse affaire,* is a prodigious rider in her own right. A model of feminine beauty, she hides beneath that surface what Balzac's narrator calls her *virago:* "Virago was hidden beneath the most feminine and seemingly weakest of surfaces. Her heart was excessively sensitive, but she held her head high with a virile resolution and a stoic firmness. . . . When one saw her white wrist, delicately shaded by blue veins, no one imagined that it could defy that of the most hardened rider."[12] At first glance, of course, we are once again in that familiar Balzacian territory of mixed genders, so often illustrated by his male protagonists. But Laurence's hidden virility takes the particular form of a propensity to travel on horseback with utmost celerity and without apparent effort: "She often rode fifteen leagues without stopping . . . and returned to Cinq-Cygne [her château] where no one could detect on her fresh face the least trace of fatigue or worry" (8:539). Clearly unfazed by the physical demands of long hours in the saddle, she also knows full well the value of a good horse properly groomed and maintained. When she takes as her groom Gothard, a young cowherd from the region of Troyes where her country estate is located, the first thing she does is to teach him how to clean and feed horses "with the care and attention exercised by the English" (8:539). Decidedly, whenever we encounter questions of horses and horsemanship in France during the first decades of the nineteenth century, English methods appear and take on almost mythical overtones as models for exacting the fullest possible performances from horses. Laurence does well to provide herself with the most rapid instruments of travel possible, because, as the reader quickly discovers, beneath the polite surface of this young woman lies a fierce partisan of the deposed monarchy. As such, she has become the messenger and the organizer of a group of émigrés hiding in German territories and planning the assassination of Napoleon Bonaparte.

Une Ténébreuse affaire begins in 1803, at a moment when Bonaparte and his police have gotten wind of a conspiracy against the person of the emperor. After having demonstrated her courage and mettle during the Terror, when she was a young girl and had to help her family face down an angry revolutionary mob, Laurence de Cinq-Cygne is now one of the principal liaisons between the émigrés and their allies in Paris and in the rest of France. Among those émigrés are Laurence's twin cousins, the Simeuse brothers, who fled during the Terror, reluctantly leaving Laurence behind. The town near Laurence's estate, Troyes, is between Paris and the German border, and the young woman circulates in this intermediate space, carrying messages and offering whatever help she can. In particular, as the novel opens, she is providing logistical support to the group of émigrés, including her twin cousins, who are planning the assassination of the emperor. She obviously needs a fast horse and the skills to ride it on long trips, often during the night, in order to escape the detection of Bonapartist spies who are implanted in the region. In a surprising twist, as a conspirator against the republic (now in its imperial form), Laurence will have to confront the same republican spy and policeman whom we have already met in *Les Chouans*, namely, Corentin. It seems that in *La Comédie humaine* whenever the circulation of secrets along the roads and paths of the republic is at stake, Corentin is never far away. Indeed, *Une Ténébreuse affaire* begins with the mysterious arrival of Corentin and his lieutenant, Peyrade, at the house of Michu, a devoted but secret protector of the Cinq-Cygne family. As the scene opens, Michu's house, on the edge of the forest near Laurence's château, is approached by two unknown men of whom Michu is instantly suspicious. It is striking to remark that both policemen are on foot in this scene and thus contrasted from the start with Laurence, whose very person is associated with riding and speed. Moreover, Corentin and Peyrade first appear in the scene at the edge of the forest, in a troubling, ambiguous space that is neither completely open (emptied of impediments like a road) nor completely closed. It is a labyrinth of passageways that can become a medium for messages, a veritable knot of paths through which travelers and messengers can and must move. Sent by Napoleon and Fouché, Napoleon's minister of police, to undo the conspiracy and to capture Laurence's two cousins, Corentin and Peyrade appear as if out of nowhere, by magic, converging on the region around Troyes under specific orders from Fouché to uncover the extent of the plot against the emperor. Their shadowy circulation through and around the forest surrounding Troyes is clearly in parallel with Laurence's own secretive movements throughout this same region.

The first half of the novel is devoted to a single day, during which Laurence discovers that Corentin and Peyrade know about the conspiracy and have come to Troyes to capture the two Simeuse brothers, her émigré cousins. She and Michu will be forced to put to work their considerable skills at moving swiftly about the region around the Château de Cinq-Cygne, in order first to find the conspirators en route to Paris before Corentin finds them and to alert them to the danger of the discovery of their plot—and then to spirit them away to safety. At dinner that evening, Laurence has just returned from a long ride designed to clear the way for the conspirators to travel toward Paris to accomplish their act. She has not yet been informed by Michu that the plot has been discovered: "Having returned only at six o'clock from the border of the Brie region, after having scouted ahead of the troop in order to allow the four gentlemen to arrive safely at the haven where they were to make their last stop before converging on Paris . . . she had sat down for dinner without changing out of her dirty riding-habit and her half-boots" (8:542). The other inhabitants of the château, the rest of Laurence's family, have become accustomed to seeing her in such a state, dirtied from riding: "All the inhabitants of the château had their own occupations; life there was as regimented as in a monastery. Only Laurence troubled the atmosphere with her sudden trips, her absences, with what Mme. d'Hauteserre called her escapades" (8:548). The staid life of the family may indeed be disturbed by the energy generated by her mysterious disappearances, but the political dimensions of those activities are apparent to no one. Laurence is quite unlike her relatives, who are prepared to accept Bonaparte and the empire and to abandon their devotion to the fallen monarchy. These differences between the rest of the family and Laurence de Cinq-Cygne are marked symbolically by the young woman's propensity for movement. She possesses a kinetic energy that disturbs the tranquillity of life after the Revolution. On this particular evening, the other members of her family have remarked that Laurence's mare is particularly tired and that her hunting rifle was not used during the trip she has made—all are signs of activities that are disquieting, albeit still enigmatic.

The evening described in the first half of the novel is, quite simply put, a race between two opposing parties: Corentin and Peyrade on one side, Laurence and Michu on the other. Both want to reach the anti-Bonapartist conspirators first. The race involves not only the movement of persons but the movement of information as well. In the first decades of the nineteenth century, the telegraph is never far removed from situations requiring rapid information exchange, as we shall see in a moment. But first, we must remark that after arriving at Michu's house on foot and conversing with him, Corentin and Peyrade make contact with the police agents of the region and quickly find a conveyance that allows them to circulate more conveniently about the region, "a wretched cabriolet made of wicker, harnessed to a post horse" (8:556). The rather sorry conveyance the two police agents use is in symbolic contrast to Laurence's sleek mare, because when she is astride her horse, Laurence is capable of maneuvering through the forest in ways that would be unthinkable in a carriage. The first proof of this comes when Corentin and a detachment of gendarmes encircle the Cinq-Cygne estate, from which Laurence succeeds nonetheless in escaping by slipping through a crack in the wall with her horse. Then she and Michu proceed to thread the needle and pass between the gendarmes spread out around the house and to gallop away without detection or pursuit: "[Michu] led the young woman at a gallop for half an hour, zigzagging, doubling back, cutting across his own path through clearings to cover his tracks" (8:562). These maneuvers recall the *crochets de lièvre* about which Maxence Gilet spoke in *La Rabouilleuse* when he was describing the kinds of maneuvers that might have allowed him to compete more successfully with Philippe Bridau and perhaps ultimately would have spared his life. To be quick, but also nimble, is of paramount importance in the scene of escape recounted in *Une Ténébreuse affaire.*

But how to get to the conspirators in time to warn them and to allow them to hide? The ultimate problem here is that whatever is to be done has to be done before daybreak, because, as Michu puts it, "The telegraph goes faster than the best horses" (8:567). Indeed, pitted directly against one another, the telegraph will always carry information more quickly than a horse—provided, of course, that the weather is clear and that the message is sent during daylight hours. The window of opportunity to save Laurence's cousins is reduced to the hours left before daybreak, while the telegraph is out of operation. Laurence has already ridden to meet the conspirators once during the early evening, to send them on their way toward Paris. Now someone must make the same ride, one which Laurence and Michu discuss:

> "My mare comes from the stables of the count of Artois, she was sired by his most beautiful English thoroughbred, but she has just run thirty-six leagues, she would die before she would carry you through to the end," she said.
>
> "My horse is a good one," said Michu, "and if you traveled thirty-six leagues, that means I only have eighteen to go?"
>
> "Twenty-three," she said, "because they have been on the road for the past five hours! You will find them beyond Lagny, at Coupvrai, from where they are supposed to leave at daybreak disguised as bargemen." (8:567)

We learn more about Laurence's horse here. If it is not a thoroughbred, it is nearly one. Sired by the English thoroughbred of the count of Artois, the mare has all the characteristics necessary to accomplish the feat required. Unfortunately, she has already been ridden a long distance earlier the same evening, and thus the only solution will be to send Michu on with his own horse. The trip will be twenty-three leagues (72 kilometers) one way. Michu will have to warn the conspirators of the danger and bring them back to hide in the region around Troyes: forty-six leagues in all.

Unable to make the trip on her horse because the mare is too tired, Laurence plays a diversionary role by riding through the forest and returning to her château, in order to induce the police agents to shadow her instead of detecting and pursuing Michu. Throughout all of her maneuvers, she is opposed by Corentin, who is perhaps fooled at the beginning, but who quickly puts two and two together. Nothing she does will dupe him in the end, and once he has understood that Laurence and Michu are attempting to get a warning message to the conspirators, he knows that his only chance at winning this contest of information speeds is to send a telegraph message: "He . . . took a notebook from his coat pocket, scribbled two orders in pencil, sealed them, and called one of the gendarmes over:

'Gallop to Troyes, wake the prefect, tell him to use the telegraph as soon as daylight permits'" (8:578). Unfortunately for Corentin, the telegraph operators will have to await daybreak to send a message up the line. There is no way to close the time gap once Michu has eluded the police and galloped away toward Paris. The only thing Corentin can do at this point is to verify whether Michu's horse is gone and, if so, to speculate about where it and its owner might be. The verification is easy, because the horse Michu uses is very particular. As one of the agents remarks, it has all the characteristics of an Arabian and is easily identifiable. This final descriptive element of the episode confirms the rule: if Laurence herself is characterized by her movement on a horse that is a descendant of an English thoroughbred, it is eminently logical that Michu, her ally, is a good rider and owns a horse out of the ordinary for the region, characterized by an uncommon speed in the service of Laurence's cause.

Laurence and Michu thus succeed in saving the Simeuse brothers and the group of their co-conspirators, but not for long. If Corentin fails here, he ultimately succeeds in capturing the conspirators as a result of a faked kidnap attempt for which he is able to pass them off as the authors. The story of how Corentin and his allies devise and apply this strategy is recounted in the second half of the novel, which I shall not treat in detail here. The conclusion to the second and final part of the novel, however, returns to the themes of overland travel and information speeds that characterize the first half of *Une Ténébreuse affaire.* After fighting for the acquittal of her cousins during their trial and failing to win that acquittal, Laurence is forced to ask Bonaparte to pardon the brothers; in other words, she is forced to confront the person who has been her mortal enemy since he came to power. To find the emperor, who has already begun his Prussian campaign when Laurence sets out to meet him, is no easy task. To await his return, however, is to condemn her cousins, who will die unless the emperor commutes their death sentences. Laurence is forced to take to the roads and must accomplish a perilous journey in pursuit of Napoleon, "who was traveling with the rapidity of lightning" (8:678). The emperor is riding the very roads that he contributed so much to building and maintaining, and which were at the center of his expansionary plans. He is leading his military machine at breakneck speed deep into the heart of Prussia. It is fitting that the only way Laurence de Cinq-Cygne can finally confront him and promise her submission to the regime is precisely on the roads, in the course of a journey where her talent for moving quickly is once more put to the test.

4 *Velocities: Precision, Overload (Dumas)*

In chapter 85 of Alexandre Dumas's *Le Comte de Monte-Cristo,* Monte-Cristo embarks on a stagecoach trip to Normandy, where he has invited Albert de Morcerf to accompany him. His intention is to remove Albert from the increasingly tense situation in Paris that has been created by Monte-Cristo's plot to exact methodical revenge on Albert's father, Fernand (now count de Morcerf). Albert's father was one of the co-conspirators who plotted to have Monte-Cristo (when he was still Edmond Dantès) thrown into prison as a Bonaparte sympathizer at the beginning of the story recounted in Dumas's novel. The passage describing the trip can serve as a reference point for any study of speed and communication that highlights the formation of a highly organized system to move messages and people more quickly during the first half of the nineteenth century in France. The narrator offers readers a veritable psychological analysis of speed and its effects on those who were encountering it for the first time:

> The journey began in a very somber mood, but it soon brightened because of the physical effect of its rapidity. Morcerf had never conceived of such speed.
>
> "Indeed," said Monte-Cristo, "With your relay system averaging two leagues per hour [equivalent to eight kilometers per hour], with the stupid law preventing one traveler from passing another without asking his permission, which means that a sick or suffering traveler has the right to force lightly packed and healthy travelers to follow behind him, loco-

> motion becomes impossible. Personally, I avoid this inconvenience by traveling with my own postilion and my own horses. . . ."
>
> And the count, leaning out the door, made a sound that gave wings to the horses. They were no longer running, they were flying. The coach swept forward with a sound of thunder on the royal pavement, and passersby turned to watch the flaming meteor pass. Ali repeated the sound made by the count, smiled showing his white teeth, grasped the steaming reins in his strong hands, spurring on the horses, whose beautiful manes blew in the wind. In the dust raised by his efforts, Ali, child of the desert, finding himself back in his element, with his black face, his fiery eyes, his white burnoose, seemed to be the very genius of the simoom and the god of the tempest.
>
> "This is a voluptuousness that I have never known," said Morcerf. "It's the voluptuousness of speed."
>
> And the last clouds on his forehead dissipated, as if the air rushing past had carried them away.[1]

Like Thomas De Quincey, who made a habit of riding on top of mail coaches to experience the feeling of speed as directly as possible, Albert, unfamiliar with the velocity that Monte-Cristo's logistical support system is capable of generating, is overwhelmed by his experience in the coach. The trip described here is presented as frankly mood-altering. Albert, who begins the trip burdened by the effects of Monte-Cristo's revenge, which was fast becoming a noose tightening around his family's neck, involuntarily gives himself over to the unexpected pleasure of going fast.[2] As this trip makes perfectly clear, speed is at the heart of *Le Comte de Monte-Cristo.* Such speed is new, it is exhilarating, it is addictive.

In "The Informatics of Revenge," a brief but suggestive article on the novel, Geoffrey Winthrop-Young makes the following statement: "*The Count of Monte Cristo* is one of the first novels to freely indulge in aestheticizing speed; it does so by depicting the physical exhilaration derived from swift motion and by celebrating Monte Cristo's 'marvelous rapidity,' be it the speed with which he travels or the 'marvelous promptitude' with which his servants execute orders." Indeed, the novel makes it amply clear that Monte-Cristo is the fastest man alive (in his period), one who is never hindered by intervals, be they calculated in time or distance. Not only can he fly, almost literally, over distances, but the precision orchestration of his arrivals is unmatched by anyone in the novel (and doubtless by anyone—fictional or nonfictional—in the period). In Rome, he strikes up a friendship with Albert de Morcerf, whose identity Monte-Cristo knows well and whom he has specifically targeted as the best entry point to begin exacting revenge on Fernand's family. Albert immediately reciprocates his favors by inviting Monte-Cristo to visit him in Paris.

The count accepts the invitation in the following terms: "Do you want to meet on this very day at this very hour? . . . I warn you that I am despairingly exact. . . . May 21, at ten thirty in the morning, at 27 rue du Helder [in Paris]" (417). Needless to say, Monte-Cristo arrives in Paris at the address on the chiming of the half hour, precisely as he had promised. Rapid movement is thus accompanied by an almost surreal exactitude. For a modern reader who has not yet analyzed the question of the movement of passengers during the 1830s, this speed and precision can only appear miraculous, yet another sign of the omnipotent and omniscient qualities with which Dumas has endowed his protagonist. We now have the requisite perspective, however, to understand that Dumas's portrait has a clear historical substructure. Moreover, we need to be well aware that such promises of preciseness in arranging meeting times and in fulfilling pledges of this sort are common in the novel. Another instance that confirms the rule can be found in Monte-Cristo's dealings with Morrel, the shipowner in Marseille who trusted him when he was young (before Monte-Cristo was thrown into prison in the Château d'If) and whose fortune the count has therefore decided to protect. In a characteristic scene, Monte-Cristo extends the time for repayment of a debt Morrel owes in terms that are quickly recognizable by any reader of the novel: "Rest reassured, sir, I will take care of everything. Today is June 5. . . . Well, extend these promissory notes to September 5, and on September 5, at eleven in the morning (the clock showed eleven o'clock at that precise moment), I will arrive at your house" (269). It is as if Dumas had purposely chosen to exaggerate this trait. Monte-Cristo's meetings are scheduled to the minute—and he never misses them. Only a master of speed and of the infrastructures of movement could make such guarantees and keep his word.

What Monte-Cristo accomplishes during his trip to Normandy with Albert de Morcerf is prodigious indeed, but it must not be seen simply as an isolated performance. Rather, it is the culmination of a considerable organizational improvement in the upkeep and development of the infrastructure of stagecoach travel before the explosion of railroad construction in France. Monte-Cristo, even with his own post horses and carriage, would not be able to travel to Normandy so quickly if the roads were not able to carry him and if the necessary organization were not already in place. Hence the reference in the passage quoted above to the "royal pavement," a part of that necessary infrastructure allowing the count's performance. Parenthetically, the description of the noise produced by the coach, "the coach swept forward with a sound of thunder on the royal pavement," corresponds to the way French eyewitnesses in the early part of the nineteenth century regularly described the noise created by the passage of mail coaches—especially during the night, when they broke the silence of sleepy provincial towns and villages.[3] A certain level of expectation about velocity and precision was already present in the stagecoach system itself. Monte-Cristo simply actualizes this potential to a greater degree. He escapes the public post relay system by creating his own relays with post horses at his beck and command, and thus he avoids bottlenecks created by certain principles of the relay legislation of the period, in particular, the notion of first in, first out. The first carriage arriving at the relay station must be serviced first, unless a mail coach arrives, which has precedence over anything but a royal carriage. Monte-Cristo's remark about the difficulties of passing slow coaches corresponds, moreover, to legislation actually in effect at certain moments during the first decades of the century, establishing the principle that coaches could not pass other coaches once on the open road without requesting permission from the coaches to be passed. There were as well prohibitions on changing horses and/or drivers between official relay stations.[4]

Dumas is not simply waxing metaphorical when he speaks of Monte-Cristo's speed and precision. The passage describing the trip to Normandy demonstrates the care with which Dumas treats important elements pertaining to the count's fortune and power. The count and Albert engage in a conversation during the trip to Normandy that furnishes the outlines of the infrastructure at stake. The horses used are all descendants of a single stallion bought by Monte-Cristo in Hungary and known for performance in its bloodline: "In Hungary six years ago, I found a famous stallion renowned for its speed; I'm not sure at what price I bought it, because Bertuccio [one of the count's trusted servants] paid for it. In the same year, it had thirty offspring. We will be using all this progenitor's descendants during the trip. They are all alike, . . . because this privileged animal of the stables gets the best mares" (915). But what will happen when the count no longer needs all these animals, Albert wonders aloud? Monte-Cristo responds that he will sell them for a tidy profit. The problem, counters Albert, is that "there would not be a king in Europe rich enough to buy them" (915). The overland travel infrastructure the count has put into place for himself is both extensive and expensive: it is clearly beyond the means of the average European monarch. The cost of the horses alone would be enough to break the bank of any ordinary ruler. Thirty-two horses comprise the group of relay animals available to the count. Divided into eight relays, they allow a performance nothing short of spectacular. The travelers cover 47 leagues in eight hours. The calculation is simple: 47 leagues is the equivalent of approximately 188 kilometers. If one divides that distance by eight hours, the result is an average speed of approximately 23 to 24 kilometers per hour. This was unheard of during the period in which the story is set. The average speed of a single galloping horse rarely exceeded 18 to 20 kilometers per hour. As Monte-Cristo himself indicates, moreover, the average speed of the normal public post coach was barely one-third of what the count can accomplish.

If the horses Monte-Cristo uses are uncommonly fast, the efficiency of his driver and of the horse team exchanges at the relays must also be quite out of the ordinary if they are not to interfere with the performance of the horses. Albert perceives this velocity to be magical, but Monte-Cristo responds: "With me, Albert, nothing is ever magical, figures and reason, that is all" (916). Nonetheless, as Albert had remarked earlier: "Decidedly, you are a man of prodigious accomplishments, and you will succeed not only in outdoing the railroad, which is not really that difficult, especially in France, but in going faster than the telegraph" (914). We shall return to the question of the juxtapositioning of stagecoach travel and the telegraph in a moment, but meanwhile the occasion should not be missed to underline how this remark calls attention to the lag between railroad construction in France and what the English had already accomplished. In France, it was not hard to travel more quickly in a stagecoach than by railway during this period, because the system was simply not yet well-enough developed. It takes more than the raw speed of the locomotive and its mechanical parts to outrun a stagecoach—a high level of organization is also required. Until the end of the 1830s in England, and slightly later in France, private coach cars circulated on railroad tracks, along with the coach cars of the larger companies that ran the lines they had built. The result was a scheduling nightmare that dramatically reduced the efficiency of the system as a whole (Schivelbusch 25–28).

Amazing feats of overland travel are characteristic of Dumas's novel from the very beginning. In the first chapters of *Le Comte de Monte-Cristo,* Villefort steals from Edmond Dantès a letter containing news of the plot to help Napoleon escape from the island of Elba and return to power (this is the origin of Dantès's imprisonment, from which he emerges as the count of Monte-Cristo). After having used the information against Dantès, Villefort also wants desperately to use it in order to increase his own political visibility under Louis XVIII's regime. He decides to go to Paris in person to let the king know about the coming invasion, and he must get there quickly if the information he possesses is to accomplish its purpose. On Villefort's arrival, one of the king's courtiers describes the speed of Villefort's trip: "My messenger . . . just finished a trip of 220 leagues in a stagecoach, and in barely three days" (85). As we saw earlier, a league equals 4 kilometers and thus the trip was 880 kilometers long. If it took seventy-two hours to complete, the average speed was just over 12 kilometers an hour. Public stagecoaches only rarely exceeded 14 or so kilometers an hour at top speed. It would be safe to say that Villefort makes it from Marseille to Paris in an uncommon time for a public stagecoach passenger, certainly as fast as one can travel during the period without making private arrangements, such as those created by Monte-Cristo. For purposes of comparison, Stendhal has Lucien Leuwen return to Paris from Nancy, some 320 kilometers, in thirty-two hours. This is another astonishing overland travel performance, as I claimed earlier, especially since Lucien has to maintain himself on horseback during the whole trip, whereas Villefort is seated inside a coach. Lucien's trip is physically taxing in a way Villefort's is not.

Dantès/Monte-Cristo's prowess on the water is also part and parcel of the context of velocity in movement established by Dumas early in the novel.[5] From the beginning of the first chapter, when the return of Edmond Dantès's ship to Marseille is described, Dumas establishes Edmond's commanding presence as navigator and master of the vessel on which he serves. His captain may have died of a fever during the return voyage described as the novel opens, but Dantès has taken over and brought the ship safely back to port. The ship's owner, Morrel, is quite prepared to name Dantès as the new captain. Years later, when he is rescued from the water by smugglers after his escape from the Château d'If, Dantès offers his services to the ship's captain and is promptly put to the test. He suggests an immediate heading for the ship that will save it considerable maneuvering time. This path, this trajectory, however, would bring the vessel perilously close to a rocky outcrop that the captain had purposely planned to avoid. Intrigued by Dantès's cocksure manner—in fact, already seduced by it—the captain proposes to let Edmond maneuver the ship in the proposed direction: "Take the helm . . . and let us judge your expertise" (197). Dantès promptly steers the vessel precisely where he had projected that it should go, handily avoiding the dangerous rock formation and obtaining the approbation of the other sailors. To navigate is to imagine trajectories in a space where none is marked. To navigate means to understand how the infinite number of points in the void of the seascape are interconnected and can become itineraries. It means, ultimately, to choose the best path for getting from one point to another in the least possible time with the least peril. Commerce on the Mediterranean dictates that times of passage be reduced to the absolute minimum possible, and Dantès is clearly an expert at this type of exercise.

No one sails faster, knows the Mediterranean better, inspires the confidence of other sailors more than Edmond Dantès. The open, uncharted seascape is a veritable transport mechanism that sweeps the count of Monte-Cristo around the shores of the Mediterranean in every direction at breakneck speed. Italy, Corsica, France, North Africa, the Middle East: wherever Dantès can sail he goes effortlessly—he can be in any place at any time. The narrative structure of the first third of the novel, in particular, helps develop this sense of ubiquity.[6] Dumas writes in the form of a series of jump cuts, some better managed than others, that take the story from one place to another without transition and thus almost without distance and interval. At every stop along the way we encounter Dantès in yet another of his incarnations—as if he existed anywhere and everywhere in the Mediterranean seascape. The narrative technique employed by the author does little to prepare the reader for these incessant breaks. Instead they take the form of a series of chance meetings that lead the reader each time to discover Monte-Cristo in yet another of his disguises, in yet another city around the borders of the Mediterranean.

It is fitting, of course, that the outlaw Monte-Cristo is able to evolve freely through the passages afforded by the Mediterranean Sea. At war with his betrayers, in fact at war with society as a whole, he spontaneously adopts the first medium of what Paul Virilio has called total war. The void, the open space of the sea, is of primordial importance in Virilio's musings on military strategies. In *L'Insécurité du territoire,* he quotes Friedrich Ruge: "The sea is where war took on its character as total war very early . . . because the power that dominates the sea *knows no contingencies nor obstacles.* . . . The indestructible sea needs no upkeep, and its spaces are all naturally linked together" (27, Virilio's italics). The ocean is a space without infrastructure, where all points are linked to all others, and where all obstacles impeding circulation are removed.[7] It is the space of *aporia,* as the Greeks called it, from *a poros,* meaning a space without passages. Within such a space the warrior can travel in any direction, toward any shore. Those who are landlocked can at best fortify the shoreline and await invasion from unseen and unpredictable enemies—unseen and unpredictable because they can arrive from anywhere and at any time across a medium of uncharted open space. This explains in part the uneasiness of Louis XVIII in the beginning of *Le Comte de Monte-Cristo,* about which more will be said in a moment, when he confronts the danger of invasion mounted by the banished Napoleon. The king cannot know when or precisely from where the actual danger will come, because the former emperor will arrive by sea at an uncertain interval. Hence, as well, the symptomatic placement of the Château d'If, a bunker in the Virilian sense of the term, within which Edmond Dantès stockpiles the skills necessary for him to leverage the vast expanse of the Mediterranean—enticingly set out before him—which he will seize when the moment is right (Virilio, *Bunker Archeology*). The Château d'If is a sentinel just off the shoreline of the port of Marseille. Those who fortify shorelines with edifices of this type are condemned to a defensive posture that cannot match the energy and unpredictability of the enterprising party who seizes control of the sea as transport medium.

A characteristic scene in chapter 32 of the novel summarizes Dantès/Monte-Cristo's affinity with the wide expanse of the Mediterranean. Marked by a particular visual perspective, the structure of the description Dumas writes in this scene could be compared to a painting whose principal characteristic is its vanishing point. After spending an evening on the island of Monte-Cristo with Albert de Morcerf's friend, Franz d'Epinay, Monte-Cristo leaves his sleeping guest and embarks on his yacht bound for an unknown destination. When Franz awakens, he hurries to the edge of the island and scours the horizon with a telescope to spot the count's boat on its itinerary toward the southern tip of Corsica. In turn, Monte-Cristo, perched aft on the deck of his yacht, uses a telescope to peer back in Franz's direction. The two looks encounter one another and the two wave goodbye, each with a white handkerchief—the only way their gestures can be perceived at such a great distance. That distance, indicated by the necessity of the telescopes without which any farewell would be impossible, is palpable. Moments later, when Franz returns for another look in the direction of Monte-Cristo's yacht, it has become indistinguishable: "When Franz came back on the beach, the yacht was only a white speck on the horizon. He tried his telescope again, but even with the instrument it was impossible to distinguish anything" (310). A simple enough moment, it would seem, but one that nonetheless turns Monte-Cristo's yacht into a point on this maritime surface, moving along at such a rate that it disappears almost before the reader's eyes. The yacht with Monte-Cristo aboard is the vanishing point of a landscape, which is, in fact, a seascape calculated visually to emphasize its expanse. The velocity of Monte-Cristo's yacht, a phenomenon that makes the count's vessel blend into the surface on which it travels, is something like the signature of Monte-Cristo's link to the medium that transports him anywhere and everywhere.

By the time the scene in question occurs in the novel, the yacht has already been recognized by the narrator as a vehicle of considerable potential. Under construction in Genoa and destined for an English lord, the vessel is bought instead by Dantès (he offers a substantially higher price than the original client). He then has the yacht fitted out to his pleasure using the first money he takes from the island of Monte-Cristo, from the treasure revealed to him by the abbé Faria in the course of their conversations while they were imprisoned in the Château d'If. Dantès sails the yacht out of Genoa harbor on its maiden voyage alone, without a crew, to the surprise not only of its builder but of all the other expert observers in the port city, who watch his departure and are deeply impressed by his skills:

> Dantès left the port of Genoa, escorted by the gaze of a crowd of curious onlookers, wanting to see the Spanish lord, who was in the habit of navigating alone [Dantès has assumed the identity of a Spanish lord during the negotiations with the shipbuilder]. Dantès passed the exercise with flying colors. With the aid of the helm, which he never relinquished, he put the vessel through the necessary maneuvers. It responded like an intelligent being, ready to obey the subtlest hint from Dantès, and he thought to himself that the Genoans deserved their reputation as the premier shipbuilders in the world. (224)

The onlookers follow the evolutions of the vessel in exactly the same fashion as Franz does from the island of Monte-Cristo—"until they lost sight of it" (224). Moreover, the trip in the yacht from Genoa to Monte-Cristo is immediately viewed as a performance, like the other coach trips we have considered: "The vessel was an excellent sailboat and covered the distance in thirty-five hours" (224).

Distances and intervals are *media* in *Le Comte de Monte-Cristo.* They are the space, the gap through which messages transit as easily as people. When Louis XVIII meets Villefort at the beginning of the novel, he immediately associates Villefort's trip from Marseille to Paris with the question of the telegraph.[8] Why, the king wonders, did Villefort take the time to come to Paris when an hour or two would have sufficed to send the information by telegraph? The coincidence between the movement of people and the movement of information that this remark highlights needs to be developed. In my reading of Stendhal's *Lucien Leuwen,* I pointed out how extensive the optical telegraph system had become by the 1830s in France. The country was blanketed by a relatively complete system of lines. It would be appropriate and important here to provide some inkling of the speed of messages sent through the system. We have treated many of the details of its structure, but until now we have only alluded to its actual speed and therefore its capacities. From the broadcasting of the first signal emanating from the point of origin of a message until the reception of that first signal at the message's destination, the following optimal time performances were possible: Paris-Lille, two minutes; Paris-Calais, just over four minutes; Paris-Toulon, just under fourteen minutes; Paris-Bayonne, twelve minutes. As telegraph historian Geoffrey Wilson asserts, if Paris-Bayonne took twelve minutes for the passage of the first signal of a message, then "a message containing 150 signals, equivalent to half a page of writing, passed in 1½ hours" (138). If one considers that it took a minimum of two to three days, and probably more when conditions were not ideal, to travel by coach from Bayonne to Paris during this period, one can begin to grasp the magnitude of the change of scale in the speed of message exchanges represented by the telegraph. Paris was linked to the major outlying regions of France with a system that allowed messages to reach the center under the proper conditions (daylight, good weather, and alert operators) in less than an hour if they were concise enough. We have to keep in mind that we are always speaking of optimal performance here, because weather and darkness could considerably slow down operations (recall that Lucien Leuwen pressed to have his first message sent from Caen without delay, in order to minimize the risk of the effects of winter fog and darkness on his transmission).

Villefort's trip to Paris is a performance from the perspective of the movement of a traveler, but it is also an ultrarapid movement of information. At stake are details about the plot to return Napoleon to power, information discovered by Villefort in the letter he confiscates from Dantès when Dantès returns to Marseille as the novel opens. The question of the telegraph comes to the fore in part because Louis XVIII cannot understand why his minister of police, who has the telegraph system at his disposition, does not know more than Villefort:

> "Let's see," murmured Louis XVIII, . . . "And how many men does he have with him?"
>
> "Sire, I do not know," said the minister of police.
>
> "How is it that you do not know? Did you forget to inform yourself of this circumstance? . . ."
>
> "Sire, I was not able to inform myself of this. The message simply bore the announcement of the landing and of the route taken by the usurper."
>
> "And how did this message get to you?" queried the king. . . .
>
> "By telegraph, sire," he stammered.
>
> "To fall from the throne," continued Louis XVIII, who at first glance had immediately measured the precipice on the edge of which tottered the monarchy, "To fall from the throne and to learn of one's fall by telegraph! . . . Ridicule: you do not know what this is in France, and yet you should know." (90–91)

A subtle dialectic develops between speed, on the one hand, and information overload, on the other. Yes, the telegraph is fast, but it is fast on the condition that the message not be too detailed. Villefort's trip was ultimately far from superfluous—it allowed for a certain triangulation of information that improved the overview of the king. Louis XVIII's reaction to the news, his prediction based on what he has heard, "to fall from the throne and to learn of one's fall by telegraph," goes a long way toward summing up the problem. The telegraph is a perfect medium when it comes to brief summaries of events, but it is a much more problematic medium when it comes to transmitting information about the complex contextual circumstances that always surround such events. The headline "Louis XVIII Deposed" would match telegraphic capacity perfectly, but the fine detail of strategy and context that gives full meaning to such a headline exceeds the capacity of the medium.

The return of the emperor, announced both by telegraph and by Villefort in person is actually an incident defined by a veritable contest of communication and information. When Villefort encounters his father, Noirtier, in Paris during this same trip, we discover that Noirtier is a Bonapartist sympathizer and activist and is thus pitted against his own son. In fact, the letter stolen from Dantès was destined for none other than Noirtier himself. The son and the father have a conversation during which they match their information about the emperor's return and ultimately boast about who is the best informed, who possesses the most up-to-date and rapid communication about the event. Says Noirtier: "You think you are well informed because a telegraph tells you, three days after the debarkation, 'The usurper has landed at Cannes with a few men. We have gone after him.' But where is he? What is he doing? You know nothing about that. He is being pursued. That's all you know. Fine, but he will be pursued all the way to Paris, and not a shot will be fired" (100). Noirtier mocks the information that the king has received and points out the very weakness about which we have spoken, namely, its necessarily incomplete nature, resulting, at least in part, from the abbreviated form that the telegraphic message must take. He claims, moreover, to be as well informed as his son—and just as quickly—through a Bonapartist parallel police system: "Believe me, we are just as well informed as you, and our police are just as good as yours. Do you want proof? Well, you wanted to hide the news of your trip from me, and nonetheless I knew of your arrival half an hour after you went through the gates of Paris. You gave your address to no one but your driver and yet I know that address. The proof is that I have come here" (100).

Noirtier, later a quadriplegic and aphasic after a massive stroke, develops his own code and message system with his granddaughter and proves once again that his existence is intimately tied to the question of codes and messages. To communicate with his granddaughter after his stroke, Noirtier blinks his eyes in an abbreviated Morse code that his granddaughter interprets. He answers "yes" or "no" to questions put to him in such a form that one of these answers is appropriate. In fact, the blinking is equivalent to a semaphore shutter system not unlike what Lantenac fantasizes about in the scene in *Quatrevingt-treize* briefly analyzed in my introduction. One of the most famous scenes mobilizing this code is the scene where Noirtier writes his will in an attempt to prevent his granddaughter from marrying Franz d'Epinay against her desire. It is not coincidental from my perspective that the description of Noirtier's communicational code is juxtaposed with an extended discussion of the telegraph system in France in the following chapter of the novel, linking Noirtier to Monte-Cristo structurally, reinforcing the bonds between the two characters.

Any reflection about the capacity of the optical telegraph system brings us necessarily back to the discussions preceding the 1837 law dealing with the ownership of the optical telegraph system, about which I spoke in the context of my reading of Stendhal's *Lucien Leuwen.* We saw how the opponents of privatization argued that the telegraph system was not well enough developed to allow simultaneous arrival of potentially conflicting news reports. The postal system did a much better job of this, the argument maintained, because numerous letters could transit simultaneously and arrive at the same destination synchronically. The opponents of privatization won the debate, and the telegraph remained under state control in order to prevent potential stock market manipulation by speculators. If confirmation or contradiction of news was not possible, given the limitations on the amount of information that could transit through the system, incomplete or false reports could be sent to influence stock market prices, only to be contradicted later, when it was already too late to prevent profit-taking by unscrupulous investors. This bottleneck in the system points to a broader conceptual problem linked to the notion of the *network.* The ambition of Claude Chappe and his brothers was ultimately to create a communication system that linked all areas of France together, and this principle was summarized and underlined by Ignace Chappe in his 1840 *Histoire de la télégraphie.* By connecting important towns all over France, the whole nation would be covered "with a telegraphic network linking all areas to one another and to a common centre. The French . . . [would] thereby benefit from the considerable social advantages provided by frequent and rapid communications" (quoted in Flichy 30). This was an ambitious project, and we would do well to reflect on the extent to which it was realized.

Patrice Flichy compares the development of optical telegraph lines to that of the French road system during the period. The ambition of the monarchy under Louis XV had been to improve a chaotic system of roads that had never been administered in a nationally unified manner. The historical document that is emblematic of the beginning of this reform is the *Instruction du 13 juin 1738,* issued by Comptroller General Orry and establishing the right of the central government to compel all districts in France to furnish the labor necessary to build and maintain the road system (Arbellot 766–67). Two successive directors of the Administration des Ponts et Chaussées (office of bridges and roads) under Louis XV, Daniel-Charles Trudaine and his son (decidedly, when one speaks about important engineers in the eighteenth century, one often encounters a family affair!), set to work to improve the system. One must not paint too rosy a picture, however, because despite evident gains in overland travel times for many destinations outside Paris, the pressures brought to bear on road development in France remained quite contradictory. On the one hand, the central government, especially during and after the Revolution, wanted a road system that rendered the country transparent and united from the center. On the other hand, provincial French citizens were much more interested in being connected to the important towns and cities in their own regions than in constructing overland communication routes opening their regions to Paris as the national political and cultural center. Flichy summarizes the situation: "While the 'memorandum on the repair of roads' in 1738 introduced a first hierarchical classification of roads, the attempt to plan an ordered and articulated network was not to materialize. Improvements were carried out on sections of roads only, and although towns were well aware of the advantages in being situated on an important road, their main concern was their connection with neighboring cities" (30). In his remarks on the development of the English road system during the late eighteenth and early nineteenth centuries, Philip Bagwell makes a related observation. The pull between local roads and the national road system occurred at the level of the *corvée,* the enforced labor of peasants and farmers, who were called upon to contribute to the building and upkeep of roads in their regions once a year. Says Bagwell: "So long as they [the local peasants and farmers] remained the principal beneficiaries from their labours there was some sense in making parishioners maintain the roads. But once the roads took on the character of thoroughfares linking distant centres of population and industry it was unjust to expect farmers and labourers to work unrewarded mainly for the benefit of strangers" (36). The rise of capitalism and the concomitant increase in the concentration of wealth had an impact on the city/country divide at the level of the national transportation systems in both France and England and exacerbated the confrontation between local government and central government.

It is instructive to compare the development of the telegraph system to that of the road system. Whereas the improvement of the road system was constantly bogged down in local debates and desires and tended to develop regionally in complex ways, telegraph construction was relatively untrammeled by such debates and politics.[9] Because the system was entirely state controlled and because the investments and compensation issues were decidedly less onerous than in the domain of road construction, the telegraph system took on a particular form.[10] As Flichy describes it: "The engineers of telegraph lines were subjected to far fewer constraints. Telegraph installations were not of the same size and local authorities' intervention was insignificant since the central government was the sole user of the telegraph. When Chappe launched a line, he had a global view of it and carried it through to completion. The Chappe brothers' network . . . (Ignace used the term in his book of 1840) nevertheless remained a group of lines from Paris to the provinces, with no connection between them" (30). The use of the term "network" is a key point of interest here. Was the Chappe telegraph system really a network in the modern sense of the word? In an important way one cannot call it a true modern network. The problem was that the lines emanating outward from their Parisian center were not linked together laterally. They were simply juxtaposed and did not therefore function in a way that could maximize their potential as a network. The Chappe brothers and their successors did ultimately realize that there was a potential gain in efficiency possible by linking the five main trunk lines that served the corners of the country from Paris. That realization came gradually along the way as the system was completed. Flichy quotes from another memorandum authored by a successor of the Chappe brothers around 1830: "There is no relation between the five lines from Paris. They are isolated, so that each of them has to be self-sufficient and can expect no help from any of the others. . . . The causes for a suspension or slowing down of transmissions (bad weather or heavy traffic) are reduced when the lines are linked . . . so that each telegraphic direction has at least two alternatives for corresponding with the centre" (30).

With an analysis of this sort, envisaging the interconnection of lines that had at first been constructed as independent entities, one begins to be able to imagine a communicational network in the modern sense. A network is by definition multiconnected, that is, information transiting within it is not confined to a single route but can take any one of multiple routes to arrive at its destination. The paths of the network are reticular, branching, and interconnected. Flichy claims that reflection on true reticular networks began in earnest in the nineteenth century and that analyses concerning the interconnection of the telegraph system parallel reflections that can be found articulated in other domains, for example, in relation to problems of water delivery in the increasingly large urban centers of the nineteenth century (30–31). The model was likely the human circulatory system.[11] The absence of multiconnection within the optical telegraph system meant that the optical telegraph was destined to fail to reach its full potential. But even if interconnection had become an integral part of the development plans of the system, one can wonder just how far network development could have progressed with the optical telegraph. If it had eventually become the case that messages had more than one path possible for moving between origin and destination, one might nonetheless wonder whether the speed of the system would actually have allowed for true networking. The optical telegraph was rapid, but it was not instantaneous. The branching, reticular structure of the telegraph system could reach its full potential only with the advent of the electrical telegraph, which was much more nearly instantaneous, so that the route taken by a message, as roundabout as it might potentially be, did not significantly slow down the transmission and thus the arrival of the message at its destination. Only the electrical telegraph would really solve the problem of incomplete information that Dumas's Louis XVIII faces in *Le Comte de Monte-Cristo* and that the French legislators of 1837 so feared.

Having fully described Monte-Cristo's expertise in the domain of rapid overland and water travel, I would claim that it should come as no surprise to discover that he is also perfectly attuned to the existence and potential of the telegraph. To put it another way, Monte-Cristo knows full well that distances and intervals are simultaneously media for messages and space and time gaps to be bridged by the physical movement of bodies. Chapters 60 and 61 of *Le Comte de Monte-Cristo* make this amply clear. The count visits a telegraph station outside Paris and bribes the operator to send a false message. Although the content of the message is not described in the novel, we do know that it causes Danglars's wife, Hermine, who is dependent for insider information on Lucien Debray, her lover, to suggest an incorrect stock market position to her husband, who thereby loses a substantial sum of money (remember that Danglars is one of Monte-Cristo's betrayers, another mortal enemy on whom Monte-Cristo exacts exquisite revenge). Lucien Debray works in the Ministry of the Interior, the very administration, we recall, that controlled the telegraph—both optical and eventually electrical—until the system's merger with the postal service, begun in 1873 and completed in 1878. The convergence of diplomacy and stock speculation in the medium of the telegraphic message is an imbrication that Monte-Cristo seems to understand effortlessly. When this comprehension is combined with a concerted effort to tap into and thus to short-circuit the medium of the telegraphic message, one can be sure that Monte-Cristo will soon reveal himself to be an expert at using the telegraph to manipulate those who depend on it.

If indeed Monte-Cristo perceives how speculation and politics exist in tandem in the telegraph network, he also possesses sufficient technical knowledge about the telegraph codes to enable him to send a false message. Those codes were first devised at the time of the system's conception in 1792–94, a moment of turmoil, as we have suggested, during which the French revolutionary state was trying to defend itself against European powers dedicated to its destruction. Small wonder that the codes were a state and military secret. They were part of a centralizing apparatus of control, the efficacy of which depended on the fact that only the strategists of the central government could transmit and decipher them. The codes were modified over time, moreover, because as experience with transmission difficulties accumulated, changes and refinements were introduced to make transmissions more efficient. For Monte-Cristo to be able to send a convincing false message, up-to-date information on the codes would be required. The narrator does not explain how the count has gotten his intelligence about them, but the clear implication is that he has an inside source and knows as much about the system as any of the telegraph inspectors who kept the system functioning at peak efficiency. And if Monte-Cristo knows about telegraph messaging, this really means that he knows all about the most advanced technologies of message-sending of his day, because the optical telegraph was the occasion for some of the most complex thinking about the techniques associated with communication over distances during the period in question. One must point out, in particular, the presence in this context of reflections about the basic flow control of messages, that is, the creation and use of codes that signified various message states (begin, stop, end, repeat, error, and so forth). It must not be forgotten, moreover, that the optical telegraph caused at least practical experimentation with human vision in order to discover the limits of what the eye could usefully discern as discrete differences in the spatial positioning of the telegraph arms—without introducing excessive errors into messages passing from one station to the next. One might also say that the optical telegraph brought about the first modern, albeit still rudimentary, reflection on data compression techniques. Without entering too deeply into the detail of the code, suffice it to say that short sequences of signals (pairs or triplets) were used to refer to column and row positions on the pages of a code book and that the resulting referencing system allowed the creation of a code that contained around nine thousand letters, syllables, words, and phrases. The reader should understand that what is at stake here is not a Morse-like code, in which words could actually be spelled out letter by letter, but a system that necessarily had to include the data compression allowed by referencing a code book containing common words, phrases, and syllables. Otherwise, the optical telegraph would have been painfully slow and considerably less useful than it actually was. Only with the advent of the electrical telegraph did messaging over distances once again approximate the flow of discourse from the hand of the writer, as the electrical telegraph operators became capable of forming words in something like a real-time writing mode.[12]

The level of sophistication in the use of codes and of message flow control that soon became apparent in the optical telegraph system can be illustrated by an incident that found its way into the newspapers in the mid-1830s in France. To understand the full implication of the episode, several elements pertaining to the coding system of the optical telegraph need to be emphasized. Operators of the telegraph stations did not know the meaning of the full set of transmission codes—they did not have and did not use the code book. Only the inspectors, stationed at divisional points throughout the system (every ten stations or so along the line), verified that messages had not been corrupted. The verification took the form of decoding and then re-encoding the messages by using the code book to which only inspectors had access. This decoding and re-encoding obviously slowed down transmission, but it served important purposes. First, of course, it minimized transmission errors by detecting them and correcting them along the way. In addition, however, it increased the efficiency of the system in times of inclement weather. If weather interrupted transmission locally, a message verified at a divisional station could always be sent via a courier on horseback to the next divisional station along the line to be re-encoded and thus to resume its transmission despite locally unfavorable weather conditions. In any case, ordinary operators simply repeated the positions of the telegraph mechanism's arms that they detected as the positions were produced by the next station up the line. They left encoding and decoding duties to the inspectors. All the lowly operators really needed to know were the flow control codes, because, of course, they had to control the flow of signals in both directions, in other words, to signal various ready states to the next operator up or down the line.

The telegraph administrative authorities did not at first realize that the flow control codes themselves could become meta-codes. For example, instead of sending the wait signal once, it could be sent twice or three times, and the repetition given a meaning for observant spies. This is a classic example of a cascading communicational system in which an operator at one level sees only random errors, whereas an operator at the next level can see information. The news item referred to above had to do with a stock fraud perpetrated by unscrupulous investors and discovered after two years in 1836.[13] A group of fraudulent speculators in the mid-1830s used a manipulation of flow control signals to organize a system of insider information. Here is a succinct description of the plot:

> A curious case of fraud was discovered on the Paris to Bordeaux line. Two bankers, the brothers François and Joseph Blanc, had bribed the telegraph operators at a station just beyond Tours to introduce a specific pattern of errors into the transmissions, to signal the direction in which the stock market was moving in Paris to an accomplice in Bordeaux. The telegraph operators near Tours received their instructions from Paris by ordinary (stage-coach) mail, in the form of packages wrapped in either white or grey paper, indicating whether the stock market in Paris had gone up or down. The fraud had been in operation for two years when it was discovered in August of 1836. (Holzmann and Pehrson)

The reason the perpetrators of the fraud had to bypass the Tours station and get down the line to the next station on the Bordeaux side of Tours is that Tours was a divisional station, where messages were purged of spurious errors. If "errors" were to make it down the telegraph line into Bordeaux, the divisional station had to be bypassed. This incident demonstrates strikingly that once a code system is adopted, sophisticated and unsuspected use of it is never far behind—coding systems are by nature cascading. It was not difficult for a third party to figure out how the flow control codes differed from the body of the message and then to devise ways to mobilize their omnipresent repetitions into a signifying system.[14] Even the lowly telegraph operator whom Monte-Cristo bribes in chapter 61 of Dumas's novel differentiates effortlessly between the codes he does not understand and those he uses to control the state of transmission at his own station (661).

One can speculate fairly confidently that when Dumas was composing *Le Comte de Monte-Cristo* in the first years of the 1840s, he knew of the affair just described or of similar scams. The technique employed by Monte-Cristo to perpetrate his own fraud corresponds quite closely, moreover, to key characteristics of the actual fraud exposed in the columns of French newspapers in 1836. Some preliminary remarks concerning the imposing presence of the telegraph edifices in the cultural landscape of the period are in order. Dumas's introduction to the episode describing Monte-Cristo's visit to a telegraph station and his subsequent bribery of the operator adds striking confirmation to our previous remarks concerning the material visibility of the optical telegraph system, which is also a key to any reading of Lucien Leuwen's experiences with the telegraph during the election in Caen in Stendhal's *Lucien Leuwen.* When Monte-Cristo informs Villefort and his wife of his intention to make a touristic visit to a telegraph station, he encounters disbelief on the part of Mme. Villefort, whereupon the count launches into a veritable dithyramb devoted to the physical appearance of telegraph stations:

> I have occasionally seen black, moving arms resembling the legs of a giant Coleoptera rising up in the air at the end of a road, on an elevated knoll, in a moment of brilliant sunshine. I have never seen such a view without great emotion, I swear to you, because I have always thought that these bizarre signs, cutting through the air with precision and carrying over a distance of three hundred leagues the unknown will of a man sitting behind a table to another man sitting behind another table at the end of the line, were outlined on the gray of the clouds and the blue of the sky by the sole force of will of some all-powerful ruler. It always leads me to believe in genies, sylphs, gnomes, in short, in occult powers—and it makes me laugh. But I never took it upon myself to look more closely at these giant insects with white bellies and black, thin legs, because I was always afraid that beneath their stone wings I would find nothing but a human genie—snobbish, pedantic, filled with science (cabalistic or sorcerous). But one fine day I learned that the motor of each telegraph station was a poor working devil, earning twelve hundred francs a year, who spends all day looking—not at the sky like an astronomer, not at the water like a fisherman, not at the landscape like an empty-headed dreamer—but rather at the white-bellied insect with black legs placed four or five leagues away from him, that is, his correspondent down the line. (654–55)

This is a striking passage indeed. The mysterious moving arms of the telegraph stations of the first half of the nineteenth century make them resemble beetles driven by some hidden force. The operator, in the belly of the beast, is invisible, and the robot-like precision of the movement of the arms is therefore in some sense inexplicable—even frightening. David Charles has shown how the view of telegraph stations elicited similar metaphorical fancies from Victor Hugo as well, which, although they contain different images, demonstrate just as clearly the suggestive power of the system's visible presence in the landscape: "A telegraph, poor wooden machine driven by a rope, was moving in the clouds and projecting through space . . . [its] mysterious language. . . . On top [of the tower of Saint-Michel], in the light and the sun, in the midst of the blue sky . . . [was] a telegraph gesticulating wildly, like Pasquin on stage" (quoted in Charles 223–24).[15]

Simultaneously, however, Monte-Cristo knows that the movement is not random, that a message is being transmitted down the line. He is surely not one to let a metaphorical moment of description hamper his analytic powers. His immediate focus is on the distance covered by the messages transmitted by the system, that is, on the very type of interval that he is an expert at bridging. We could well imagine that his fascination with the distance traveled by the messages derives from his own almost fetishistic attention to travel and precision over vast distances. What he discovers ultimately upon reflection, moreover, is the weak link in the whole system, namely, its poor, largely uneducated operators. For all its potential, the telegraph's integrity as a network for message transmission depends on the work accomplished by its numerous operators along the lines. Perhaps they do not know what they are transmitting when they manipulate their station's arms, but without them, without their dedication to the job they are doing, the system would immediately be compromised. The rules and regulations governing the behavior of the operators were strict. Under the administrative prescriptions for the functioning of the telegraph, any mistakes or carelessness by a local operator drew an immediate sanction and fine and, if repeated, led to his dismissal. Monte-Cristo's plan, then, is to attack the system at its weak link, at a station beyond the divisional terminus in Paris. When Villefort hears of the count's desire to visit a telegraph station, he immediately assumes that Monte-Cristo will visit the station at the Ministry of the Interior or at the Observatory in Paris. To pass a false message, however, requires that Monte-Cristo escape the decoding operations of the terminus or of any other divisional station and intervene at a simple repeating station. This strategy corresponds precisely to the one adopted by the fraudulent speculators who established themselves as parasites on the Bordeaux line in the mid-1830s. They, too, suborned a simple repeating operator, poorly paid and poorly educated, and thus turned the telegraph to uses unanticipated by state authorities.[16]

It is perhaps not useful to enter into the detail of Monte-Cristo's transactions with the operator of the Montlhéry station on the Bayonne line (the same line, in fact, on which the 1835–36 Bordeaux stock market fraud had been perpetrated). Suffice it to say that chapter 61 of Dumas's novel reads like a treatise on the operation of one of the typical repeating telegraph stations in the system. The operator informs Monte-Cristo of many of the rules and regulations concerning the station and its functioning, elements that could have been found in any operator's manual of the period—proof, if further proof is necessary, of Dumas's extensive familiarity with telegraph operations during the first half of the nineteenth century in France. The attack on the integrity of the system perpetrated by Monte-Cristo suggests some further remarks on the network's structure, however. At first glance, this state-owned communication system, consisting of a series of towers distributed along lines reaching out toward the provinces, takes the form of a series of impregnable bunkers. These resembled fortified citadels, whose location on high ground or in towers not only served the purpose of projecting signals as far as the eye could see but replicated as well a system of military fortifications that had long been a mainstay of a highly centralized political structure in France.

One could imagine, then, that the optical telegraph system was composed of more than five hundred small forts broadcasting signals that only the state authorities could understand, each station capable of being defended in time of trouble by a relatively small detachment of soldiers. A priori, the model seems eminently safe and relatively immune to political upheavals. And yet, as Dumas (through Monte-Cristo) demonstrates in the wake of the stock market frauds of the 1830s, these fortified bunkers were, on the contrary, eminently vulnerable. The concentration within the telegraph towers all over France of the secrecy of the codes, on the one hand, and of fortified, protected state space, on the other, had the unexpected effect of rendering the system susceptible to intrusion. The vulnerability resulted from the fact that each isolated repeating tower was manned by a semi-ignorant operator, whose loyalty depended entirely on his desire to protect a job that paid poorly, the conditions of which were less than inviting (an omnipresent responsibility to maintain a ready state during daylight hours and not to slow down transmission under any circumstances). If we reflect carefully on the much more distributed nature of the subsequent electrical telegraph network, we can see how the electrical telegraph shows unsuspected strengths against disruption and intrusion. Despite early fears that electrical telegraph lines were too exposed in times of trouble, thereby making the act of cutting wires and shutting down the system too easy, the proliferation of electrical telegraph lines and their multiconnectivity worked powerfully against such an eventuality. It ultimately mattered little that lines could be cut locally, because messages could transit without interruption through other parts of the network, provided that redundancy and interconnectivity were sufficiently developed. Moreover, repair of such intrusions was a very simple affair.

The sending of state secrets in the codes of the optical telegraph system contained another hidden vulnerability. If the code itself is understood by its users to be a state secret, there is little immediate incentive to modify it or, for that matter, to turn it into a system of ciphers ever more sophisticated and constantly evolving to foreclose any deciphering, detection, or tampering. A closed system of this sort induces one to think much more in terms of protecting a given state of the code than in terms of developing the cipher to make it eventually more efficient and more difficult to break. It suffices, one thinks, to prevent others from being able to use it. In such a context, once criminals or interested parties obtain copies of the code, by theft or bribery, they are instantly privy to secret messages throughout the whole system. And that system, heavily invested in the existing codes (because they are part of its smooth and rapid operation—they are simultaneously codes and a rudimentary type of data compression), could only be extremely slow in responding to such a breach. Once Monte-Cristo bribes the operator at Montlhéry to send a false message and thus breaches the system, the count need only pull out of his pocket a sheet of paper that contains the stolen signs and then instruct the operator to insert them into the message flow. He thereby instantly has access to the whole line on which the message is transiting: "Monte-Cristo pulled out a piece of paper on which there were signs traced, and numbers indicating the order in which they were to be formed" (663). The system is in some sense completely transparent to such a gesture. Once the later electrical telegraph system was in place, however, ciphers proliferated and gave rise to a veritable science that would know its ultimate heyday during the Second World War (Rosenheim). Not only did multiconnectivity provide a better distributive network than was the case for the separate, poorly interconnected optical telegraph lines, but the proliferation of encoding created a new and more complex "theory" of secrets. International telegraph committees tried at first to ban the use of codes on the electrical telegraph network, but this became impractical almost immediately. If ordinary language can itself become a code very easily, precisely who will ultimately judge whether any given ordinary sentence is actually "ordinary," or, on the contrary, a hidden cipher? (Standage, especially 105–26). Private users began at once to encode messages, not only to protect their confidentiality but to compress them as well, since telegraph messages were paid for by the word and were expensive to send. Under such a different set of circumstances, Monte-Cristo might well have encountered a multilayered encoding system that would have posed a more complex set of problems for accessing the message flow and inserting a viable false message.

The preceding remarks were meant to underscore the fact that the optical telegraph is an extremely curious mixture of the old and the new. On the one hand, it had many characteristics of modern systems of telecommunication. Flichy lists them in his discussion of the Chappe telegraph: "Although not instantaneous, transmission was extremely fast. . . . A permanent network was constituted which spread further and further afield. . . . A specialized technical body took over the operation of the network. . . . Information was coded in a 'universal language.' Chappe had integrated operational constraints in the communication system by defining operation signals . . . which were distinct from correspondence signals" (31–32). On the other hand, the model of a series of bunkers conceived as citadels meant to protect the transmission of a code, which was itself a state secret, has undeniable connections with an older, traditional model of state power. The explosive growth of the subsequent electrical telegraph network was destined to modify the relations between communication and state in extremely fascinating ways. A modern theory of communication arose at the beginning of the twentieth century in the wake of a new system of message transmission (the electrical telegraph), itself already caught up in a profound mutation provoked by the rise of the telephone and, subsequently, of wireless communications. Ultimately, the building of the optical telegraph was an instance where the development of a new communicational system was less the result of any new technological invention (the theory of semaphore transmission of messages was not new at the end of the eighteenth century) than it was the result of a series of political developments that reorganized national space in France and that thereby actualized the potential hidden in existing communicational technologies, as we have already suggested.

Here the parallel with the development of the road and stagecoach relay system is instructive. As we have seen, the technological developments that led to more efficient and rapid road travel in stagecoaches were not revolutionary, they were evolutionary. The introduction of speed and precision scheduling in overland travel had much more to do with an organizational effort to realize potential efficiencies contained within existing technologies (better management of road construction and repair, better organization of the relay system, better suspension systems for the stagecoaches themselves, and the like) than with any striking new technology. The development of overland speed was under way before the technological break of the steam engine and the railroad and before an even later technological break, the gasoline engine. Likewise, the optical telegraph mobilized the potential of a series of existing technologies and imagined a first communicational network before the invention and perfecting of the transmission of electrical signals over wires. But clearly it was a hybrid system—not quite a network in modern terms (lacking multiconnectivity) and built like a series of mini-fortresses that harked back to an older state organization.

Before we leave the episode of the false telegraph message recounted in chapters 60 and 61 of *Le Comte de Monte-Cristo,* another element, one that crowns the whole incident, needs to be foregrounded. We have seen that the speed of the telegraph transmission had implications for the way receivers of the messages had to react to them. Lucien Leuwen's minister, M. de Vaize, sends Lucien running to his father with buy or sell orders based on insider information, and the effectiveness of the strategy depends on the fastest possible action once de Vaize possesses the relevant news. This situation is faithfully reproduced in *Le Comte de Monte-Cristo,* as Lucien Debray, who works at the Ministry of the Interior, attempts to leverage the information he has received from Monte-Cristo's false message: "Five minutes after the telegraphic news had arrived at the ministry, Debray ordered horses to be harnessed to his carriage and ran to Danglars's house" (664). Once Mme. Danglars has been informed of the news and grasped the implications for the stock market, she runs to her husband, "who, in turn, ran to his broker and ordered him to sell at any price" (664). The time is so short that any attempt to take some distance from the news, to analyze it and weigh its possibilities, is precluded. Losses or gains are swift and great. In this case, between the losses he takes by selling his stock very quickly and the higher price the stock finds once the news upon which the operation was based has been revealed to be false, Danglars is out a million francs. Increased speed brings exponentially increased risk, just like increased speed in stagecoach travel and then rail travel brings accidents that are ever more violent and mortal. Philippe Bridau had already discovered this at the end of Balzac's *La Rabouilleuse,* when he risked his fortune on the stock market with bankers whose goal was to ruin him. The rapidity with which he can accomplish speculative operations ultimately induces him to gamble heavily on the basis of insider information and propels losses that put an end to his immediate ambitions and that far exceed what might have occurred in a historical period when information transited more slowly.

Monte-Cristo knows about the telegraph and the communication technologies it spawned. Almost from the beginning of the novel, after all, he is an expert at data compression and manipulation, largely because he has a mentor who teaches him the necessary techniques. As Geoffrey

Winthrop-Young has argued convincingly, the abbé Faria is a true artist when it comes to distilling the essence out of data. He has developed an exceptional mental concentration that is ultimately the result of the constraints placed on him by his solitary confinement. Once Dantès and Faria are able to work together and to communicate, the abbé spends his time imparting this valuable knowledge to his pupil. Dantès's mind is a blank slate when he enters the Château d'If. He is clearly marked by his intelligence and energy as the novel opens (he seems, after all, prepared to assume the responsibilities of being captain of the vessel on which he sails, despite his extreme youth), but he is completely unformed in any intellectual areas outside his special gifts as a navigator. Faria takes on the task of teaching his method to Dantès. During the prison episode, the characteristics of Faria's method are demonstrated most particularly by the riddle of the text indicating the existence and location of the treasure hidden on the island of Monte-Cristo. Faria spends years unpacking this message and brings to bear on its decoding all of his intellectual gifts and experience. Readers of Dumas's novel will recall that Faria discovered the secret of Cardinal Spada's fortune when he lit a piece of paper in the fire in order to rekindle his candle, only to discover that the paper to which he had just set fire actually contained a secret ink that became visible when heated. Unfortunately, part of the message on the paper burned before Faria realized what was happening, turning the text into a code that had to be deciphered: "From what was on the remaining fragment, I guessed at the rest by measuring the length of the written lines against the length of the paper and by penetrating the hidden meaning using the visible meaning" (173).

The preceding remark highlights both the material and the intellectual aspects of the involuntary data compression at stake here. The message has been foreshortened materially by fire and must be expanded—first using a material algorithm, namely, the size of the letters and the standard length of the lines. In addition, however, filling in the blanks in any cogent manner will require the invention of a bridge from the apparent meaning revealed in the writing that remains visible toward the hidden meaning of the writing that has been effaced. The meaning of the visible marks must be expanded, more widely contextualized, and this expansion depends on the invention of a complex algorithm of analysis and understanding. The processing of the message contained in the text is an emblematic demonstration of the abbé's wide intellectual powers derived from the method of concentrated analysis that has become his hallmark. Cut off from any access to the immense store of human knowledge he once possessed materially (let us not forget that he owned a very large library in his previous life, for instance), Faria spends his solitary confinement in prison analyzing his knowledge and reducing its unmanageable richness to an essential core. That core is, in fact, his own analytic capacity to expand from a bare minimum of content to encompass a broad and profound part of human knowledge. The algorithmic method he perfects during his years of confinement had actually begun to take form even before the abbé's imprisonment: "In Rome, I had around five thousand volumes in my library. By reading and rereading them, I discovered that with one hundred fifty well-chosen works, one possesses if not the complete summary of human knowledge, then at least everything that it is useful for a man to know" (145). His technique for learning languages corresponds perfectly to this strategy. He explains, for example, how he is learning modern Greek even though the field of examples available to him is very small, since he has no new material from which to work in prison: "Yes, I made a vocabulary list of the words I know. I arranged them, combined them backwards and forwards, so that they can suffice to express my thought. I know about a thousand words. That's really all I need, even though there are, I think, a hundred thousand in the dictionary. Yes, I would not be eloquent, but I would make myself perfectly understood" (145–46).

It is not at all surprising that in the course of his conversations with Dantès, one of the problems upon which Faria exercises his considerable analytic powers is the enigma of Dantès/Monte-Cristo's imprisonment. Left to his own devices, Dantès makes no progress in determining why he was thrown into the Château d'If with no hope of being liberated by the authorities. When the abbé finally listens to the young man's story of the events leading up to his imprisonment, he responds to Edmond's narration of the events with what he calls a maxim: "If you want to discover the guilty party, first look for the person who stands to gain the most from the crime that has been committed" (150–51). Faria's "maxim," however, is not really a maxim in the seventeenth-century sense; it is not a moral commentary on a certain psychological behavior. Rather, it is a simple analytic rule that allows him to parse a series of mysterious facts and incidents that led up to Dantès's imprisonment. One might immediately suggest that Faria's technique is related to that of the detective, especially in light of the fact that the novel was written in the early 1840s, when Edgar Allan Poe was writing the first detective fiction.[17] A science of traces and deductions was fast becoming the preferred method for making sense of causal chains that assembled apparently disparate phenomena, what one might call a statistical reasoning that extrapolates from large quantities of data whatever correlations can be used to interconnect them. Faria's reasoning can be seen as semistatistical: establish a table, he intimates, and rank the gains that the various players can expect by imprisoning Edmond Dantès. The player who tops the graph in such a table is the one who holds the key to the mystery.

In short, Faria has become an expert at the techniques of data compression—he can pack and unpack at will. He has discovered the power of the algorithm. In a society that was progressively marked by an increase in the quantity of information available in any decision-making context, techniques for extrapolation were fast becoming essential. Much has been written in recent years about the fact that the nineteenth century saw a striking rise in the use and analysis of statistics, that is, information gathered with an ever finer analytic mesh, information that was becoming increasingly the crux of policy decisions and of social and economic understanding in the developing Western nations.[18] Extrapolation from vast sources of data is part and parcel of a new science. Earlier in our argument the notion of information overload played a constitutive role in imagining how quantities of information, rapidly transmitted, quickly created bottlenecks in the optical telegraph system, blockages that made it difficult to triangulate, to verify news, and to act accordingly. But the optical telegraph was poised on the brink of a new type of overload: the exponential growth of the electrical telegraph network would soon create the capacity for transmitting at high speeds altogether too much information for practical, quick, and objective analysis. How to process that information and use it effectively? Answering this question is abbé Faria's task. Within the confines of the belly of a bunker, the Château d'If, removed from any interference originating from outside his prison, the abbé develops a system for extrapolating commonalities of behavior and knowledge that can then be applied to the vast expanses of the Mediterranean world outside the bunker. When Dantès escapes the bunker, becomes Monte-Cristo, and sets forth on his quest for vengeance against those who imprisoned him, he is equipped with a mental conditioning and a method for analysis that give him an edge in synthesizing an ever denser store of knowledge. One might say that his mastery of time and distance, the physical movement of his body through space and the movement of messages through that same space, corresponds very closely to the synthetic and analytic powers of his mind, which allow him to make instantaneous jumps, to bridge intervals, to fill in gaps, and therefore, in general, to reason with a perspicacity demonstrating the types of skills that permit mastery in an age of empire.

Monte-Cristo easily grasps the essence of the optical telegraphic messaging revolution, which contains simultaneously a rupture of scale in the speed of transmission compared to anything that preceded it and, as I have insisted, a necessary engagement with the problem immediately created by the new potential for speed, namely, information overload. If a single signal transits through the optical telegraph system at breakneck speeds, nonetheless as soon as the number of signals increases substantially in order to convey complex and detailed messages, the system bogs down and surrenders part of the very speed gains it creates. If telegraph historian Geoffrey Wilson's calculations are correct, a half-page message, containing around 150 signals, sent from Bayonne to Paris, took somewhere around an hour and a half to transmit. Under the best of conditions only about a dozen hours of transmission time were available per day (the optical telegraph worked only during daylight hours, despite the hope—never ultimately realized—that some system of night signaling could be devised). One can immediately grasp how little information can be sent in the time at the disposition of the system's operators. This is the origin of the overload problem to which Louis XVIII falls prey in *Le Comte de Monte-Cristo.* The king rapidly knows of the emperor's return because of the telegraph, but he does not know enough to help him counter the invasion. The telegraph message says nothing about the number of soldiers who accompany Napoleon or about the number of sympathizers who might rise up to follow him once he has landed—or, for that matter, about various other details that would be of crucial strategic significance. Herein lies the fundamental difference between Monte-Cristo and Louis XVIII: using his fabulous wealth, the count has built for himself a communicational infrastructure that exceeds anything the French king is capable of constituting. The gathering and dissemination of messages, as well as the ultrarapid movement of his own person, give Monte-Cristo an omnipotence so clearly related to his ubiquity that one could easily say they are one and the same. Monte-Cristo is the man from nowhere, as his hashish dreams that take him out of this world symbolically underline. In the guise of a melodramatic novel of revenge, Dumas created, in fact, one of our first nineteenth-century portraits of empire, empire as it came into being in its nineteenth-century guise: a network of communication that brought together far-reaching and disparate regions of the globe under the controlling power of nation states that held the monopoly on the telegraph lines and the archives.

Conclusion: Speed Kills (Zola)

While concentrating on the historical period after the Revolution and before 1850, before the extensive development of the railway system in France, I have wanted to demonstrate that an infrastructure for—and an expectation of—speed and precision in communication were steadily created and implemented prior to the sustained expansion of the railroad system. The developing organizations permitting a more efficient movement of people and messages had a very evident impact on a series of novels by Balzac, Stendhal, and Dumas. The novels analyzed in previous chapters reflect technological developments in the domain of communication at the level of their themes, but they are also more profoundly structured by them. Balzac superimposes a family network on a stagecoach road network in *Ursule Mirouët* and gives new meaning to the narrative topos of the encounters provoked by coach travel in *Un Début dans la vie.* Stendhal constructs *Lucien Leuwen* as a diptych organized by the relation between horsemanship and the optical telegraph. Dumas gives Monte-Cristo a ubiquity that can be explained ultimately only by the communicational network at the heart of *Le Comte de Monte-Cristo* and of which the protagonist is a constructor and master. It is indisputable, nonetheless, that the social transformation in the transporting of people and messages that I have described in key novelistic texts took a quantum leap forward when the construction of railroads and of the electrical telegraph system in France and other Western European countries began in earnest. What is added by the new technological infrastructures of train and electrical telegraph? How do they change the face of speed during the second half of the century?

Although I cannot answer those questions in detail here, it would be fascinating to conclude the argument proposed in the present essay with a taste of what was to come after stagecoach service and the optical telegraph had reached the limits of their potential. And it would be hard to find a better way to do this than to turn an analytic gaze toward Émile Zola's great novel on the railroad, *La Bête humaine.* Published in 1890 (after it had been serialized in 1889–90), at a moment when the railway system was a fact of life on the social and cultural landscape of France, the novel is fully plunged into the world of speed created by the railroad during the Second Empire, particularly during the 1860s. It can provide us with a sense of the effects of speed created by the future of the organizational transformations whose beginnings I have been tracing. *La Bête humaine* creates a veritable kinetic frenzy. It is a novel in which the organization of overland travel has attained a speed that quite simply disconcerts its characters—it renders them ecstatic: it creates situations in which they are beside themselves. If madness in one form or another is at the heart of the story, that madness is directly related to speed, which has reached cinematic proportions in the novel.

My association of the kinetic with the cinematic has to do with the common root of the two terms, the Greek *kinein,* meaning "to move," and with the way in which Paul Virilio weaves the two notions together in his treatment of the beginnings of cinema in the first twenty-five years of the twentieth century. In his *Guerre et cinéma I: Logistique de la perception,* Virilio claims that the true vocation of cinema is to mobilize speed and motion in the cinematic image. Early cinema had not yet made the break with theater in its visual presentation of scenes, but this was destined to change with the Futurists. Virilio traces this change by proposing a reading of three or four key years in the career of D. W. Griffith. Griffith came to Europe toward the end of the First World War to make a film about the war that was meant to glorify the effort undertaken by the European allies—in order to stir their recalcitrant American partner into more committed action (the film was ultimately entitled *Hearts of the World* and was released in 1918). He had just triumphed with his preceding film, *Birth of a Nation,* which contained battle scenes filmed in the summer of 1914. Certain camera techniques used by Griffith to film those scenes had their artistic source in the theatrical tradition. His camera was for the most part fixed and pivoting, and it shot the movements of the troops in panorama as they unfolded before the fixed camera. One of the most difficult parts in the realization of the battle scenes in *Birth of a*

Nation was to organize the synchronized movements of a vast number of extras who had to pass before the camera with the precision of a ballet. A whole system of semaphore signaling was required to arrange the timing and flow of these sequences. What Griffith discovered to his surprise when he came to prepare the battle scenes for his new film on the European war was a static battlefield, one that had nothing to do with what he had imagined in *Birth of a Nation.* The static, stationary nature of the battlefields in the north of France was completely useless for cinematic purposes. There was nothing cinematographic about trench warfare: the two sides hardly ever moved, except under cover of darkness; in addition, the whole terrain had been swept clear of all natural obstacles and visual reference points by the constant shelling. It resembled a desert much more than a battlefield. Visual cues that might allow the battlefield to be understandable in image form simply did not exist. Griffith was forced to retreat to England, where he organized his film around a fictitious battlefield, created artificially for his needs, and where he once again used the techniques he had developed for *Birth of a Nation.*

Griffith's disappointment when faced with the static panorama of modern warfare, an organization of space that showed him—symbolically at least—that certain of his cinematographic techniques were already obsolete, was subsequently matched by what he discovered while viewing the Italian filmmaker Giovanni Pastrone's *Cabiria,* which had first been released in Europe in 1914, at around the same time as *Birth of a Nation.* Says Virilio, "With Pastrone, as with the Futurists, we encounter the end of the linear, Euclidean organization of thought and the creation of a coincidence between human vision and vehicular speeds" (21). Virilio continues: "The systematic use and abuse of the *carello* (traveling shot) that Pastrone had perfected showed that the camera serves less to produce images . . . than to manipulate and falsify dimensions. . . . The primary difference between cinema and photography is that the point of view can be mobile and can escape the stagnation of focusing and posing in order to be fused with vehicular speeds" (21). When one combines the fascination of the Futurists for vehicular speeds with the experiment of mounting a camera on one of those vehicles in rapid movement (automobile or train or airplane), one has quite simply created a new treatment of cinematographic space. The camera is transformed into an endoscopic eye, as Virilio calls it. It is projected through space, deforms space, loosens its volumes, and thus creates sensations in the spectator that are very far from the stability of the fixed eye of a camera that does not move freely and rapidly. Virilio suggests that Pastrone's experiments, prompted by the Futurist aesthetic, allowed one to imagine an aesthetic vocation for cinema different from both theater and photography. The ingredients of this transformation are movement and speed. They are effective precisely because they profoundly reorganize the visual perception of the spectator. At stake are no longer spectators who passively contemplate an action that unfolds before them and that gives them time to reflect on and to organize what they see by using ordinary visual and spatial categories. On the contrary, now spectators are almost literally projected into the action, at high speed, and the deforming of space, the loss of control over the sensations thus produced, deprives spectators of the possibility for critical distancing. This is why Virilio links the new cinema of speed and movement so closely with the rise of modern propaganda techniques, because the manipulation of vision in order to break down critical thinking was at the heart of the Nazi and the Allied war efforts.

This analysis of speed and movement in cinema is extremely pertinent to Zola's *La Bête humaine.* In any case, this novel and other Zola novels have traditionally been viewed as cinematic, but not for the same reasons and in the same sense.[1] From a narrative point of view, the first two chapters of *La Bête humaine* are characterized by the use of a protocinematic type of parallel editing. Two narrative threads that have at first glance nothing to do with one another (chapters 1 and 2 of the novel) are presented in sequence, but their narrative chronology is in parallel, so that when one arrives at the end of the second chapter, the two separate narrative threads suddenly and unexpectedly coincide at the moment of a murder, thus establishing striking thematic and structural links between them. The first chapter recounts the short stopover of Roubaud and his wife Séverine in Paris, where Roubaud discovers the past sexual liaison between Séverine and one of the railroad presidents, Grandmorin, and where Roubaud arranges for Grandmorin's murder. The second chapter, in an outwardly unrelated way, recounts Jacques Lantier's visit to his Aunt Phasie at La Croix-de-Maufras, on the railway line between Paris and Le Havre, where Jacques is tempted once again by his murderous impulses and nearly kills Phasie's daughter Flore. These two sequences intersect in the scene of the discovery of Grandmorin's body lying beside the tracks, near La Croix-de-Maufras. La Croix-de-Maufras functions as a narrative crossroads, and the discovery of the corpse there at the end of the second chapter, linking the two sequences developed in the first two chapters, thus marks a second beginning point of the story.

But we need to be more precise in the description of the junction between the two narrative sequences in question. In fact, it takes place before the discovery of the corpse—at the precise moment of the murder itself. Jacques, who has just left Flore after nearly strangling her and who is completely unnerved by the experience, wanders in the countryside around La Croix-de-Maufras and winds up next to the train tracks at the entrance to the tunnel at Malaunay. Here is Zola's description of the moment, which is a description of Jacques's perceptions as he witnesses the murder:

> Jacques first saw the black mouth of the tunnel light up, like the mouth of an oven. . . . Then the machine burst forth in the din it brought with it, in the blinding light of its great round eye . . . whose fire bored a hole through the countryside. . . . Suddenly the train cars followed, the small square windows of the doors, violently lighted, with the compartments full of passengers filing past at such a vertiginous speed that the eye doubted afterwards the images that had been glimpsed. And Jacques, very distinctly, in this precise quarter of a second, through the flaming windows of a coupé, caught sight of a man who was holding another man overturned on a seat and was planting a knife in his throat. . . . Transfixed, the young man followed the train with his eyes as the roar died down. . . . Had he seen right? And he was hesitating now. He no longer dared to affirm the reality of this vision that had appeared and disappeared in a flash.[2]

The black hole of the tunnel is a screen upon which a series of images are projected during this scene. And the projector is the locomotive itself, which surges out of the empty darkness at high speed, bringing with it a brilliant headlight that pierces the countryside and deforms the dimensions of the night. Suddenly, the bright lights of the train car windows surge forth as well, composing another series of frames, lit up in cadence, almost as if the surfaces of the side walls of the passenger cars between the windows played the role of the shutters of a projector, creating on the retina of the observer an effect similar to the one produced by an actual projector in the darkness of the movie theater. In the profound confusion of the sensations of the observer (Jacques Lantier), a hidden desire—that may or may not be a real event—is projected (in the double meaning of the term—onto a screen, outside of Jacques's psyche). One may put things as follows: the conditions of psychological absorption and fascination experienced by the cinema spectator are brought together in this episode. A moment strangely resembling the experience of participation in the moving image is created, mimicking what happens in a darkened movie theater.

The episode fuses together in admirable and striking fashion the key elements of Virilio's analysis: speed, movement, an endoscopic warping of space—in short, true cinematic vocation. What is more, a veritable fetishistic fascination hovers about the scene, because it has already virtually occurred in the text of the novel before it actually happens. In the course of his wanderings during the evening, Jacques had stumbled once before upon the tracks at the Malaunay tunnel, where a rehearsal for the scene about which we have been speaking takes place—without the explicit presence of all the essential ingredients: "Then, after having roamed over the hills for many long minutes, he saw in front of him the round opening, the black mouth of the tunnel. A train coming up the hill plunged into it, screaming and whistling, leaving behind itself a long shudder that the earth drank in, trembling" (4:1042). The reader has to wait for the second rendition of the scene before all the necessary elements fall into place. Missing from the first encounter with the tracks at the Malaunay tunnel are the windows of the passenger cars functioning as frames upon which (through which) images appear. But this missing element also occurs in Zola's text before the final moment of the murder, that is, disconnected from the moment when Jacques sees the fatal act as a series of images projected on a screen. While Lantier is visiting his aunt earlier in the evening, the conversation between the two characters is interrupted for several seconds by a passing train: "The train passed by in the violence of a storm. . . . Despite the speed, through the lighted windows of the doors, a vision had appeared of full compartments, lines of ordered heads, tightly packed, each one with a profile. They followed one another, disappearing . . . in the midst of the rolling of the cars, the whistling of the machines, the tinkling of the telegraph, the ringing of the bells!" (4:1035). We are at the heart of the problematic of speed, movement, and vision that characterizes the theoretical approach to the cinema experience that Virilio sets out in his work.

The claim that the scene holds a fetishistic fascination for Zola is confirmed by the fact that it is recounted in its entirety a second time in the novel, in the eighth chapter, from a radically different perspective—from Séverine's point of view. After having fallen in love with Jacques Lantier and become his mistress, Séverine cannot stop herself from confessing to him her role in the murder of Grandmorin—a confession that occurs in the bedroom where the project was conceived with her husband, Roubaud, before its execution in the train to Le Havre. The confession provokes the beginning of a process that will prompt Jacques to murder Séverine later in the novel, at the very place, La Croix-de-Maufras, where the murder of Grandmorin occurred. The repetitions and spatial convergences in Zola's novel give the story a deeply structured foundation. What is particularly interesting in Séverine's rendition of the events, which had previously been described by the narrator and are now presented in her personal version, is the explanation of how she and Roubaud committed the murder and then regained their seats in their own compartment in another car of the train, unobserved and while the train was traveling at full speed. The two accomplices, Séverine and Roubaud, get out of the train when it stops in Rouen and arrange to encounter, as if by chance, Grandmorin, who is traveling alone in his own private car at the very end of the train.[3] Séverine and Roubaud then get into Grandmorin's car at his behest, unseen by any other passengers or railroad employees. Once the train sets off from Rouen, Roubaud plunges his knife into Grandmorin's throat while Séverine holds Grandmorin down as the train comes out of the Malaunay tunnel, where Jacques, by chance, is crouched, after having stumbled upon the tracks a second time in the course of his wanderings around the countryside at La Croix-de-Maufras.

To avoid being accused of the murder, Roubaud and Séverine must imperatively regain their own original compartment and seats without being seen—before the train stops in the next station, Barentin, several minutes later. They do this by making their way up the length of the train to their own compartment while the train is traveling full speed down the tracks. But they must make their trek *outside* the train, using the running boards attached to the outside of the passenger cars that allow employees to reach compartments while the train is moving, all the while holding on for dear life to the thin bar affixed to the outside of the train cars to help employees accomplish precisely what Roubaud and Séverine undertake. Séverine's description of this feat is striking and compelling:

> And I found myself outside, on the running board, with both hands grasping the brass railing . . . carried along by the vertiginous flight, whipped by the wind that blew like a tempest. My hair came unknotted, I thought that my stiffened fingers were going to slip off the railing . . . glued against the side of the cars in the swirl of my skirts. . . . It seemed to me that a storm had taken hold of me, was blowing me along like a piece of straw. . . . Behind me, the countryside flew by, trees followed me in an enraged gallop, pivoting about themselves, twisted, each one crying out fleetingly as I passed. (4:1203)

The cockpits of vehicles traveling at high speeds produce strange and new effects, Virilio suggests in *L'Horizon négatif* (145–48).[4] The scenery going by outside the vehicle is divided into two distinct regions. The first, off in the distance, seems not to move at all. The second, the part that is closest to the cockpit, goes by at a speed that blurs all distinctions and details, with a physical violence that the senses have difficulty processing. Inside the cockpit, however, protected by the shell of the vehicle hurtling along at high speed, the driver/passenger is isolated from the exterior and thus from the brutal effects of the passing scenery, the closest part of which would otherwise literally assault the senses. The effects of this rapidly passing scenery are attenuated and tend to become confused with the instrument panel. They are projected onto the windows or windshield of the cockpit like a virtual heads-up display. Séverine, on the contrary, is obliged by her deed to leave behind the comfort of the cockpit and to confront directly the effects of the high speed of the moving vehicle, which is projecting her through space. The vertigo of velocity, the violent storm of the rushing wind, the swirl of her skirts, the countryside speeding by, the mad galloping of the trees, twisting, turning: Séverine clearly undergoes the experience of the close-up perception of the endoscopic space created by the lens eye of the camera strapped to a vehicle hurtling at high speed through the countryside. Even more, Séverine *is* the very camera fused to the projectile.[5] If one can say that Jacques Lantier undergoes the phenomenological experience of the creation of a space of cinematic absorption when he sees the train emerging from the tunnel of Malaunay, Séverine undergoes a related experience when she becomes, almost literally, the camera itself hurtling through the countryside, thus creating the effects of cinematic space, a space which comes into existence only by freeing the camera to probe it at unnatural velocities. Jacques Lantier sees what Séverine Roubaud records visually—he is the spectator and she the camera.

Suddenly the relationship between Jacques and Séverine becomes deeply logical, unavoidable, inevitable. Their conjunction at the Malaunay tunnel was already motivated partially by the cinematic structure of parallel editing that underlies it (chapter 1 is devoted to Séverine, chapter 2 to Jacques). But now one must further add that Jacques Lantier himself, by virtue of his position on the platform in the locomotive he controls, regularly becomes a camera lashed to a high-speed vehicle, that is, regularly experiences precisely what Séverine experienced on the night of the murder. Michel Serres has argued convincingly in *Feux et signaux de brume* that the two sources of thermodynamic energy (hot and cold reservoirs) are inscribed upon the body of the train engineer Jacques Lantier: heat from the locomotive's boiler bakes his back, the cold air from the wind he must face in order to guide the locomotive through the night freezes his face and chest (131). One can inflect this analysis in another direction in light of the preceding remarks, however. As a train engineer, Jacques is obliged to lean out of his high-speed vehicle in order better to see his trajectory and to prepare for eventual maneuvers. The following passage describes one such moment in the novel: "Jacques . . . leaned out to the right, to see better. . . . He remained there with his face in the wind, his skin whipped by thousands of pinpricks. . . . From time to time, he drew his head inside to catch his breath, . . . then he returned to his observation post in the teeth of the hurricane. . . . Twice he hallucinated and saw brief sparks the color of blood, spots on the pale curtain that trembled before him" (218). The reader should recognize instantly the parallels with the description of Séverine's experience as she tries to climb toward her compartment after Grandmorin's murder: whipped in the face by a hurricane, pushed toward hallucinations (hallucinations that correspond to the deformed perceptions Séverine experiences as trees whip by at high speed, for example), Jacques undergoes the same types of spatiotemporal deformations of perception provoked by the mad velocity of his vehicle. He experiences the effects of becoming, like Séverine before him, the eye of the camera lashed to a projectile.

A profound logic of conjunction between Jacques and Séverine is thus created in the novel—the experience of murder linking them together is part and parcel of the perceptive troubles provoked by excessive speed. Simultaneously, a structure of complete disjunction is set up between Lantier and Phasie's daughter Flore, the woman who was at first destined to be his bride. She is the polar opposite of Séverine. Flore ultimately provokes the catastrophic accident that halts the speeding train when she places a block of granite on the tracks to ambush Jacques and to arrest the movement of the endoscopic camera eye in a spectacularly violent collision. But this is precisely the reason for the disjunction between Jacques and Flore and the impossibility for them to become a couple: she cannot move through space like Jacques and Séverine; she can only throw herself across the tracks in a desperate attempt to slow down the camera, to stop the vehicle. She never learns that life when joined to the railroad becomes simultaneously cinematic and kinetic and thus lethal to those who cannot travel at top speed (but lethal as well to those who can). Ultimately, whatever argument one might make about psychological impulses, the unconscious, and madness in order to explain the relational configurations that mix together Jacques, Séverine, and Flore in *La Bête humaine,* an additional structural component in the novel always returns to trump all the others: speed and its effects. Small wonder that Jacques and Séverine constantly travel up and down the line, ostensibly, perhaps, to find time alone in Paris away from Roubaud. I would argue, however, that the trips themselves, the incessant movement to which the two characters are subjected in their repetitive itinerary, bring them ever back to the veritable force that fuels their mutual fascination for one another: speed. Flore's immobility is her downfall, and ultimately that of Jacques and Séverine as well. By thrusting a huge block of granite onto the tracks, she attempts to put a stop to things. Later, when her culpability becomes obvious, she has no recourse but suicide in the very tunnel where Grandmorin's murder took place and by a means that reinforces her symbolic position in the story. She throws herself against a train speeding toward Le Havre, crushed once and for all by the inexorable velocity of the machines that have now replaced the horses she is so adept at mastering and controlling.

Real Time, my odyssey across a series of manifestations of the effects of speed on realist narrative structures and on the representations of social life within realist novels, began with a reading of Balzac's *Ursule Mirouët.* In the course of my analysis of Balzac's novel on the *maître de poste,* I referred to Thomas De Quincey's memoirs describing his experiences riding on mail coaches in England at the beginning of the nineteenth century. De Quincey wrote about the exhilaration created by the experience of sitting atop the mail coach as it flew over the roads and spread news across the English countryside. Later I drew attention to a scene in *Le Comte de Monte-Cristo* in which the speed of a coach became a remedy for depression, dissipating clouds of melancholy through the experience of being whisked across Normandy at breakneck speed. My odyssey finishes here with *La Bête humaine,* and clearly Zola's novel provides a penetrating look from a more problematic perspective on the effects of speed. The cinematic fascination at the heart of the experiences of Jacques and Séverine hints at a darker side of speed, at its unsettling results. In fact, as overland travel speeds increased, passenger unease and anxiety increased, as Wolfgang Schivelbusch has claimed so luminously. Zola understood that madness and murder were lurking within accelerated performances of velocity. The overload we encountered so explicitly in *Le Comte de Monte-Cristo* in the context of the telegraph is thus more than a blockage in an information network; it is also a psychological manifestation of speed, which at its human limits threatens mental stability and discernment—and thus creates a space for disastrous (even murderous) accidents.

De Quincey regretted the speed of the railroad, because it no longer allowed passengers to experience physically the reality of speed. It required, instead, that they be insulated, placed in protected interiors, and thus disconnected from the space through which they were crossing. But one can be insulated only to a certain extent. After the murders of Grandmorin and Séverine, and in the wake of Flore's suicide, the runaway train roaring into the black night in the last sequence of *La Bête humaine* suggests that the dangers of speed are not only omnipresent; they are already historically well on their way to becoming a fundamental social characteristic in Zola's day. More than a century after Zola and more than a century and a half after Balzac, Stendhal, and Dumas, we find ourselves caught in the dilemmas posed by speed and instantaneity almost every day, both in our movements (often vehicular and at high speeds) and in our relation to information. What I have tried to show in *Real Time* is that the story of how we learned to live so fast extends back at least two centuries and can be seen as a central characteristic in the rise of modernity. Several of the greatest novelists in the nineteenth-century French tradition chronicled the importance of that central characteristic by making it operative and visible at the heart of some of their most fascinating fictional texts.

NOTES

Introduction

1. The national fascination in both France and England for certain notorious criminals at the end of the eighteenth and beginning of the nineteenth centuries is both reflected in and fed by the increased speed of information exchange at the beginning of the nineteenth century. On the importance of the optical telegraph for developments in the stock market, see chapter 3.

2. My thanks to Nelly Furman for reminding me about this passage in Hugo's novel.

3. Hugo, *Oeuvres romanesques complètes,* 1313. The novel was published in 1874. All translations are mine throughout unless otherwise indicated.

4. See chapter 4.

5. The configuration of the French system, which instead used windmill-like arms, will be discussed in chapter 3.

6. Jeffrey Mehlman's wonderfully suggestive reading of the same scene in his *Revolution and Repetition* uses the scene's structure for other purposes—quite convincingly, to my mind. My own interest in the scene has more to do with how it functions as a cultural marker for the shared social experience of seeing telegraph towers in operation. These structures and their workings were highly visible during the period.

Chapter 1: Webs

1. *Ursule Mirouët,* 3:774. The novel appeared in serial form in 1841 and as a volume in 1842.

2. Likewise, a few years later (1851–53), Charles Dickens writes a scene in *Bleak House* in which Mr. Boythorn is scandalized by the tardiness of the stagecoach bringing Esther Summerson and her guardian to Lincolnshire: "'By Heaven!' said he, after giving us a courteous greeting, 'this is a most infamous coach. It is the most flagrant example of an abominable public vehicle that ever encumbered the face of the earth. It is twenty-five minutes after its time, this afternoon. The coachman ought to be put to death!'" (263). Strong words indeed for some twenty-five minutes of variance with the schedule—and a clear indication that preciseness was a cultural expectation in such a situation.

3. Turgot's personal intervention was short-lived, because he ran afoul of corporatist interests, which contributed to his fall from power within a year after the reform he attempted. Many of the ideas he had floated, however, were the basis for progressive reforms in the stagecoach transportation system in the years following his first attempted restructuring.

4. In her article "La Dynamique familiale dans *Ursule Mirouët* de Balzac," Claudie Bernard analyzes the various questions—hereditary and sociological—that are raised

by this inheritance and links these questions to the notion of the circulation of goods in this provincial bourgeois society. Armine Kotin Mortimer's "Balzac's *Ursule Mirouët*" is an excellent discussion of the legal problems that underlie the struggle for the inheritance in question.

5. Père Anselme was one of the best-known *ancien régime* genealogists.

6. Thierry Bodin demonstrates the complexity of bourgeois genealogies in *La Comédie humaine,* as well as the importance attributed to them by Balzac, in an article dealing especially with *Les Paysans,* "Généalogie de la médiocratie dans *Les Paysans.*"

7. Madeleine Ambrière-Fargeaud, an editor of the Pléiade edition of *Ursule Mirouët,* informs us that this neologism is formed from the Latin word "cognomen," meaning "surname."

8. Need one point out that Minoret-Levrault occupies the place of the parasite that Michel Serres described in *Le Parasite*?

9. Ambrière-Fargeaud notes that the administrative regulation dealing with the situation in which the doctor finds himself, namely, the possibility of at least two different itineraries leading to the same destination, gives the passenger the choice of routes: "When there are two routes to the same destination, the *maîtres de poste* must respect the freely expressed desire of the travelers to take one or the other of the routes" (3:1551). Ambrière-Fargeaud further notes that Balzac takes liberties here with the road geography of the period, because the itinerary going through Nemours represents an unjustified detour in the doctor's return to Paris and thus would normally not even have been an option. The exercise of a choice by the passenger is, of course, a moot point here, since the doctor is asleep.

10. The postrider accompanying the doctor would normally have been familiar with the terrain and able to decipher whatever markers were present.

11. See Wolfgang Schivelbusch's *Geschichte der Eisenbahnreise* for an analysis of the effects of speed on the psychology of the first railway passengers. See also the discussions of these matters by Paul Virilio in *L'Horizon négatif.*

12. One need look no further for a preliminary explanation of the "retro" fascination for convertible roadsters that has taken the auto industry by storm during the past decade.

13. It should be pointed out that *malle* in French and *mail* in English come from the same medieval origin, namely, an Old French or Germanic word meaning bag or pouch.

14. In considerably more cramped circumstances than a modern traveler would accept, although, on second thought, our contemporary airline companies seem intent on re-creating nineteenth-century travel conditions.

15. The novel was serialized in 1841–42 and published in volume form at the end of 1842, the same year as *Ursule Mirouët.*

16. The verb *rabouiller* means to stir up the water in a stream or a pond in order to capture crayfish or other aquatic species. The novel's title, *La Rabouilleuse,* is the noun form of this verb and refers to Flore Brazier because she is engaged in this activity when Jean-Jacques Rouget sees her for the first time in the story. By metaphoric extension, one can also say that the term *la rabouilleuse,* always associated with Flore Brazier thereafter, insidiously suggests her attempts to muddy the waters of Rouget's inheritance.

17. Recall, for example, Eugène de Rastignac's gambling episodes in *La Peau de chagrin.*

18. See "Balzac's Gamblers" in my *Circumstances,* 155–93.

19. As we shall learn below, to be "at the heart of political life" means essentially to have access to optical telegraph messages before anyone else.

20. The description of the July 1830 revolution as a stock market speculation here

is an interestingly ironic construct by Balzac that says a great deal about his position on the results of that "revolution."

Chapter 2: Intersections

1. The novel was serialized in 1842 and published in volume form in 1844.

2. It is remarkable to note that one of the few comments about the railroad in *La Comédie humaine* refers explicitly to the disasters inevitably accompanying high-speed travel, for which precision technologies are absolutely necessary and in the course of which any breakage to a key technological component causes accidents of a scope unheard of previously: "Science, the justice system, and the public are investigating a thousand reasons for terrible railroad catastrophes caused by the rupture of an iron bar, of which one of the worst examples is the Bellevue accident" (*Splendeurs et misères des courtisanes,* 6:822).

3. The second chapter of Charles Dickens's *Tale of Two Cities* (1859), entitled "The Mail," gives a graphic description not only of winter mud but of the uncertainties of night travel in an era of highwaymen (the end of the eighteenth century) (3–9). When the mail coach described in that chapter arrives in Dover, the narrator comments: "A mail journey from London in winter was an achievement to congratulate an adventurous traveler upon" (13). Despite the improvements to the infrastructure of land travel from which Pierrotin benefits, winter travel was still hardly less adventuresome.

4. Pierrotin is not without worries for his business and has invested heavily in protecting his route by ordering a new, modern coach that will increase the comfort of his passengers. The financing of this new purchase is a crucial element of the story's opening, a moment where the business of carrying passengers and that of carrying messages intersect in an extremely symptomatic way. We shall return to this point shortly.

5. Vale, *The Mail-Coach Men of the Late Eighteenth Century,* 1. De Quincey's text can be found in 4:288–89 of the edition of De Quincey's works referred to earlier.

6. Here and elsewhere in our discussion, it must be understood that mail coaches assumed part of the job of transporting passengers in both England and France and that their interaction with other coach organizations and companies created a complex set of resonances. Later, we shall come back to the question of the mixing together of letters and people in the transportation system of the first half of the nineteenth century.

7. Hence the impatience of the mail guard in Dickens's *Oliver Twist,* to which I referred in my introduction.

8. The essay originally appeared as *Relais: Geschichte der Literatur als Epoche der Post, 1751–1913* (Berlin: Brinkmann and Bose, 1993).

9. Kittler, *Discourse Networks, 1800–1900* and *Gramophone, Film, Typewriter.* The first was published as *Aufschreibesysteme* (Munich: Fink, 1985) and the second as *Grammophon Film Typewriter* (Berlin: Brinkman and Bose, 1986).

10. See Vaillé, *Le Cabinet noir.* A history of this "institution" is fiendishly difficult to write, as Vaillé points out, because it was never established officially in any document or regulations—although it functioned continuously for more than two centuries.

11. Recent worries about security on the Internet are the modern manifestation of an ancient anxiety over the privacy of messages. In early modern Europe, during the Renaissance, when the foundations of modern postal systems were being built, cryptography was already becoming an important art and technique, as government rep-

resentatives and diplomats were attempting to maintain secrecy in the exchange of privileged information they knew was exposed during its transit in the postal system. For a recent treatment of the rise of cryptography in the modern period starting in the middle of the nineteenth century, see Rosenheim, *The Cryptographic Imagination.*

12. John, *Spreading the News,* 77. John mentions the highly entertaining memoirs of one of the early special agents of the postal service, James Holbrook, *Ten Years among the Mail Bags.*

13. Mr. Bucket, Charles Dickens's detective in *Bleak House,* traces the path of Lady Dedlock or, rather, her double, in her flight from London by querying the personnel at each relay post along her route—until he loses the trail and realizes that the lady's double has struck out across the countryside, leaving the stagecoach route, in short, that she has fooled him temporarily (814–17).

14. Philippe Mustière has argued that the narrative in the novel is structured by a series of chance encounters and incidents in the beginning. By the end, however, there is no more space for the aleatory in a society that has aligned itself with mediocrity and thus provoked the disappearance of differences and originality. See his article "Sur *Un Début dans la vie.*" Another of Balzac's short novels of the same period, 1841–42, *Albert Savarus,* returns to the themes of the transportation of people and of messages in terms that are similar to *Un Début dans la vie.* Franc Schuerewegen has written an elegant and convincing chapter on the novel in his *Balzac contre Balzac,* where he develops the theme of the purloined letter in quasi-Derridian terms.

15. The novel was published in 1829.

16. This is a pun in French on the expression *route nationale,* meaning those crucial roads that had been designated as the backbone of the road system in France and whose upkeep was in part the responsibility of the central government.

17. A quick reminder of the etymology of the term *faubourg: foris* ("outside") the *bourg* ("the city"). Although Paris has obviously grown by absorbing various faubourgs, which have often retained their designations as faubourgs despite their incorporation into the city, the term nevertheless refers to the original status of such neighborhoods—not quite yet a part of the city—and has a clear significance here.

18. Balzac, *Le Père Goriot,* 3:51. The novel was serialized in 1834–35 and published in volume form in 1835.

19. See Serres, *Hermes,* especially 39–53. The "bridges" here are symbolic and topological ones, not necessarily the physical bridges that join together the banks of the Seine at various points in the city.

20. See, in particular, in Certeau's *L'Invention du quotidien,* the chapter entitled "Marches dans la ville," 171–98.

Chapter 3: Performances

1. Stendhal, *Lucien Leuwen,* in *Romans et nouvelles,* 1:920. See also 1:922 and 1:940. The novel, written between 1834 and 1836, was never completed and was not published during Stendhal's lifetime. Modern editions have resulted from careful work with Stendhal's manuscripts.

2. See my *Circumstances,* 91–99.

3. Henri Martineau's decision to insert the text devoted to Lord Link between two chapters describing a crucial encounter between Lucien and Mme. de Chasteller in Mme. d'Hocquincourt's salon, thereby interrupting the flow of this important scene, was not retained by Henri Debray and Michel Crouzet in the 1982 edition of the novel in the Garnier-Flammarion series. The text is placed in an appendix instead, because

it has no logical position in the chapter sequence. The fragment on Lord Link, although symptomatic and crucial for my argument, might well have disappeared had Stendhal actually published *Lucien Leuwen* and thereby been constrained to make final corrections. I would add that the Garnier-Flammarion edition provides a useful running commentary in the notes on the editorial difficulties posed by the manuscript materials left by Stendhal.

4. It is hard to resist calling attention to the symbolic implications of the English lord's name, Link, that is, what joins, what serves as a connection in a communicational system.

5. New only for the French. The thoroughbred had been bred in various forms in England since the third century, when the first horses at the origin of the line were imported into England from North Africa.

6. Notice that Virilio's notion that the rider is "levitated" reproduces the sense of Lucien's remark about Lord Link's horse, which seems to float along above the ground, propelled by an almost elastic force.

7. The reader should be reminded that Stendhal planned a novel in three parts but never wrote the third part. The novel thus ends on this note of bankruptcy and raises implicit questions about the political power of the new breed of banking capitalists, a power that, precisely, provides Lucien with the only forum for public life that is available to him in the July Monarchy period.

8. Appleyard, *Pioneers of Electrical Communication,* 274.

9. See Carré, "Chappe—Innovations and Politics in 1793 and 1794." All the standard histories of the French telegraph system emphasize the link between the beginning of the construction of the system and the dangers confronting the young republic. See also Appleyard, *Pioneers of Electrical Communication,* 265–70, as well as Wilson, *The Old Telegraphs,* 121–24.

10. The term "énarque" refers to graduates of the École Nationale d'Administration, the most prestigious French institution of higher education for the formation of public servants, who often occupy high posts within the French national government administration after attending the school (regardless of political affiliation, it must be added).

11. The French term *dépêche,* one must recall, comes from the verb *dépêcher,* to hurry.

12. *Une Ténébreuse affaire,* 8:537. The novel appeared in both serialized and volume form in 1841.

Chapter 4: Velocities

1. Dumas, *Le Comte de Monte-Cristo,* 914–15. The novel was serialized from 1844 through 1846 and appeared in multivolume form in an original edition dated 1845–46, although the first volumes of this edition actually appeared in 1844.

2. It should be said that at this point Albert is completely unaware that the travails visited upon his family are of Monte-Cristo's doing.

3. See, for instance, Belhoste, "La Poste aux chevaux."

4. See Cavaillès, *La Route française,* 229. This did not prevent racing and illegal passing on the roads, which led to occasional spectacular accidents.

5. Says one Dumas critic, "The tutelary element in *Monte-Cristo* is not the air, but rather the sea. It fills the novel, and both the hero and the novel owe their existence to it. . . . The sea's presence is concrete, visible, highlighted" (Jan, *Alexandre Dumas, romancier,* 113).

6. Isabelle Jan says something comparable, but with a different emphasis: "Monte-Cristo . . . nevertheless draws part of his powers from his ubiquity. He is the man with numerous houses, and thus he does not really possess a home" (84–85). I would insist much more on the notion of trajectories than on the idea of houses and places of rest.

7. Of course, there are storms, straits, and reefs that can threaten the unwary navigator. But the fundamental characteristic of ocean travel is the open space of the seascape that permits a ship to go anywhere, untrammeled by governing bodies, strongholds, or the like—provided, of course, the navigator knows how to sail with the requisite velocity.

8. The reader should be reminded that Albert de Morcerf's exhilaration during his trip to Normandy in Monte-Cristo's coach makes him immediately associate the speed of his body with the speed of a telegraph message.

9. We have seen how the complexity of the road system is the basis for Balzac's analysis of provincial communicational systems in *Ursule Mirouët.*

10. One needs to remember that questions of public investment are always relative. While it is true that construction of telegraph stations costs considerably less than construction of roads, it was nonetheless expensive enough to be a partial reason for the demise of the optical telegraph system. The construction of electrical telegraph lines, linked at first to the construction of railroad lines and thus provided with a sort of automatic right of way, was considerably less onerous. This is especially the case when one considers that the eventual privatization of the electrical telegraph and its subsequent use by private citizens generated revenues for maintaining and extending the system.

11. Daniel Parrochia gives a considerably more complex rendering of the origins of the notion of network, which is at the heart of contemporary scientific and technological thought, in his *Philosophie des réseaux.*

12. One should not, of course, minimize the importance of the shorthand writing mode of electrical telegraph messaging, which developed from the start, but it remains nonetheless true that electrical telegraph writing was much closer to "real time" writing with a pen or stylus than optical telegraph writing.

13. The coincidence of the discovery of this fraud with the debate on the 1837 law maintaining the telegraph as a state monopoly is significant. It is safe to assume that the repercussions of the scheme had an influence on the positions assumed by certain legislators at the time of the debate.

14. Illegally tapping into the electrical telegraph system and the early telephone system was only marginally more difficult. See McMahon, *Loving Little Egypt,* for a fascinating description of telephone communication thieves in the early twentieth century.

15. Pasquin was a famous comic actor of the period.

16. A history of technology perspective on these matters would underscore the fact that the system of repeating operators, subject to verification by inspectors in every tenth station or so, was also an economic choice. To man the optical telegraph system with operators who did not need to understand the codes meant to hire only semieducated employees, who could be paid less than the more educated personnel required to run a system in which each station operator would have had to understand the whole coding system. Investment strategies and coding strategies are imbricated to an extraordinary degree here. If each individual telegraph operator had understood the whole coding system, the codes themselves would have taken a quite different form. It would be fascinating to compare this labor organization to the one created for the electrical telegraph system. One might begin with the suggestive observation that Thomas Edison began his career as a telegraph operator, subsequently working his way

up the hierarchy by dint of his intelligence. Clearly, we would not be talking about the same type of people.

17. See my "Everywhere That Marie Went," as well as my "Marque, trace, pistes." See also Winthrop-Young, who compares Faria to the later Sherlock Holmes.

18. See, for instance, Porter, *The Rise of Statistical Thinking.*

Conclusion

1. A short list of filmmakers who adapted Zola's work would include Jean Renoir and Claude Berri, of course, but also Antoine, Marcel L'Herbier, Marcel Carné, René Clément, Julien Duvivier, and Fritz Lang.

2. Zola, *La Bête humaine,* 4:1046–47. The sheer physical violence of the passage of a train at high speed and the assault on the senses that it represents are already captured graphically by Charles Dickens in *Dombey and Son* (1846–48). In chapter 55, Carker, destroyer of Dombey's wealth and of his family, flees when discovered and finds himself in a hotel next to railroad tracks. As Carker wanders along the tracks, a train passes: "A trembling of the ground, and quick vibration in his ears; a distant shriek; a dull light advancing, quickly changed to two red eyes, and a fierce fire, dropping glowing coals; an irresistible bearing on of a great roaring and dilating mass; a high wind, and a rattle—another come and gone, and he holding to a gate, as if to save himself!" (872). The violence of the experience is directly related to death, as is the case in Zola. The very night of his arrival Carker will commit suicide by throwing himself in front of a train, drawn irresistibly by its speed and power, sucked into its path by a fascination with its violence.

3. Grandmorin is in the train because Roubaud had forced Séverine to write him a note implying that she might be ready to renew the sexual liaison she had with him as a teenager. In other words, the chance encounter on the *quai* in Rouen has little chance about it.

4. Virilio picks up in *L'Horizon négatif* on remarks made by Schivelbusch about the train as projectile in *The Railway Journey* (45), although he does not refer to Schivelbusch.

5. This is something like the experience Thomas De Quincey described when writing about the English mail coach. He insisted, however, that the speed of the train later precluded the possibility of undergoing the very experience Séverine undergoes only out of desperation.

WORKS CITED

Appleyard, Roland. *Pioneers of Electrical Communication.* Freeport, N.Y.: Books for Libraries Press, 1968.

Arbellot, Guy. "La Grande mutation des routes de France au milieu du XVIIIe siècle." *Annales: Économies, sociétés, civilisations* 28.3 (1973): 765–91.

Bagwell, Philip S. *The Transportation Revolution from 1770.* London: B. T. Batsford, 1974.

Balzac, Honoré de. *Albert Savarus. La Comédie humaine.* Ed. Pierre-Georges Castex et al. Bibliothèque de la Pléiade. Paris: Gallimard, 1976–81. 1:889–1020.

———. *Les Chouans ou La Bretagne en 1799. La Comédie humaine.* Ed. Pierre-Georges Castex et al. Bibliothèque de la Pléiade. Paris: Gallimard, 1976–81. 8:857–1211.

———. *Un Début dans la vie. La Comédie humaine.* Ed. Pierre-Georges Castex et al. Bibliothèque de la Pléiade. Paris: Gallimard, 1976–81. 1:715–887.

———. *Le Père Goriot. La Comédie humaine.* Ed. Pierre-Georges Castex et al. Bibliothèque de la Pléiade. Paris: Gallimard, 1976–81. 3:1–290.

———. *La Rabouilleuse. La Comédie humaine.* Ed. Pierre-Georges Castex et al. Bibliothèque de la Pléiade. Paris: Gallimard, 1976–81. 4:247–541.

———. *Splendeurs et misères des courtisanes. La Comédie humaine.* Ed. Pierre-Georges Castex et al. Bibliothèque de la Pléiade. Paris: Gallimard, 1976–81. 6:393–935.

———. *Une Ténébreuse affaire. La Comédie humaine.* Ed. Pierre-Georges Castex et al. Bibliothèque de la Pléiade. Paris: Gallimard, 1976–81. 8:483–695.

———. *Ursule Mirouët. La Comédie humaine.* Ed. Pierre-Georges Castex et al. Bibliothèque de la Pléiade. Paris: Gallimard, 1976–81. 3:733–988.

Belhoste, Jean-Louis. "La Poste aux chevaux." <http://www.perso.infomie.fr/jomave/poste.htm> (December 30, 1999).

Bell, David. *Circumstances: Chance in the Literary Text.* Lincoln: University of Nebraska Press, 1993.

———. "Everywhere That Marie Went: Poe on the Trail of Marie Rogêt." *Oxymoron: Annual Thematic Anthology of the Arts and Sciences* 1 (Spring 1997): 140–47.

———. "Marque, trace, pistes: Balzac à la recherche d'une science des indices." In *Balzac ou la tentation de l'impossible.* Ed. Raymond Mahieu and Franc Schuerewegen. Paris: SEDES, 1998. 107–12.

Bernard, Claudie. "La Dynamique familiale dans *Ursule Mirouët* de Balzac." *French Forum* 24.2 (May 1999): 179–202.

Blanc, Louis. *Lettres sur l'Angleterre.* Deuxième Série. Paris: Librairie Internationale, 1866.

Bodin, Thierry. "Généalogie de la médiocratie dans *Les Paysans.*" *L'Année balzacienne* (1978): 91–101.

Carré, Patrice A. "Chappe—Innovations and Politics in 1793 and 1794." The Optical Telegraph: Proceedings of a Symposium Held in Stockholm, June 21–23, 1994, at Telemuseum. <http://www.telemuseum.se/historia/optel/otsymp/Home.html> (March 5, 2000).

Cavaillès, Henri. *La Route française. Son histoire, sa fonction: Étude de géographie humaine.* Paris: Armand Colin, 1946.

Certeau, Michel de. *L'Invention du quotidien I: Arts de faire.* Collection 10/18. Paris: Union Générale d'Édition, 1980.

Chappe, Ignace. *Histoire de la télégraphie.* Le Mans: Richelet, 1840.

Charles, David. *La Pensée technique dans l'oeuvre de Victor Hugo.* Paris: PUF, 1997.

De Quincey, Thomas. *The English Mail Coach. De Quincey's Works.* Edinburgh: Adam and Charles Black, 1863. 4:287–352.

Derrida, Jacques. *La Carte postale: De Socrate à Freud et au-delà.* Paris: Flammarion, 1980.

Dickens, Charles. *Bleak House.* Oxford: Oxford University Press, 1996.

———. *Dombey and Son.* London: Penguin Books, 1985.

———. *Oliver Twist.* London: Penguin Books, 1966.

———. *A Tale of Two Cities.* New York: Bantam Books, 1981.

Dumas, Alexandre. *Le Comte de Monte-Cristo.* Ed. Claude Schopp. Paris: Robert Laffont, 1993.

Flichy, Patrice. *Dynamics of Modern Communication: The Shaping and Impact of New Communication Technologies.* Trans. Liz Libbrecht. London: Sage Publications, 1995.

Holbrook, James. *Ten Years among the Mail Bags; or, Notes from the Diary of a Special Agent of the Post-Office Department.* Philadelphia: Cowperthwait and Co., 1874.

Holzmann, Gerard J., and Björn Pehrson. "The Early History of Data Networks." AT&T Bell Laboratories and Royal Institute of Technology. 1993. <http://www.it.kth.se/docs/early_net/> (March 5, 2000).

Hugo, Victor. *Quatrevingt-treize. Oeuvres romanesques complètes.* Ed. Francis Bouvet. Paris: Jean-Jacques Pauvert, 1962. 1293–1440.

Jan, Isabelle. *Alexandre Dumas, romancier.* Paris: Les Éditions Ouvrières, 1973.

John, Richard R. *Spreading the News: The American Postal System from Franklin to Morse.* Cambridge, Mass.: Harvard University Press, 1995.

Kittler, Friedrich. *Discourse Networks, 1800–1900.* Stanford, Calif.: Stanford University Press, 1990.

———. *Gramophone, Film, Typewriter.* Stanford, Calif.: Stanford University Press, 1999.

Lévy-Leblond, Jean-Marc. *L'Esprit de sel: Science, culture, politique.* Paris: Seuil, 1984.

McMahon, Thomas. *Loving Little Egypt.* New York: Penguin Books, 1988.

Mehlman, Jeffrey. *Revolution and Repetition: Marx, Hugo, Balzac.* Berkeley: University of California Press, 1977.

Mortimer, Armine Kotin. "Balzac's *Ursule Mirouët:* Genealogy and Inheritance." *Modern Language Review* 92.4 (October 1997): 851–63.

Mozet, Nicole. *La Ville de province dans l'oeuvre de Balzac. L'Espace romanesque: Fantasmes et idéologie.* Paris: SEDES, 1982.
Mustière, Philippe. "Sur *Un Début dans la vie:* Jeu du hasard, espace de l'occasion, roman de l'intempestif." *L'Année balzacienne* (1982): 195–209.
Parrochia, Daniel. *Philosophie des réseaux.* Paris: PUF, 1993.
Petot, Jean. *Histoire de l'administration des ponts et chaussées: 1599–1815.* Paris: Librairie Marcel Rivière, 1958.
Porter, Theodore M. *The Rise of Statistical Thinking, 1820–1900.* Princeton, N.J.: Princeton University Press, 1986.
Rosenheim, Shawn James. *The Cryptographic Imagination: Secret Writing from Edgar Poe to the Internet.* Baltimore: Johns Hopkins University Press, 1997.
Schivelbusch, Wolfgang. *Geschichte des Eisenbahnreise.* Munich: Carl Hanser Verlag, 1977.
Schuerewegen, Franc. *Balzac contre Balzac: Les Cartes du lecteur.* Toronto: Les Éditions Paratexte, 1990.
Serres, Michel. *Feux et signaux de brume: Zola.* Paris: Grasset, 1975.
———. *Hermes: Literature, Philosophy, Science.* Ed. Josué Harari and David Bell. Baltimore: Johns Hopkins University Press, 1982.
———. *The Parasite.* Trans. Lawrence R. Schehr. Baltimore: Johns Hopkins University Press, 1982.
Shannon, Claude, and Warren Weaver. *The Mathematical Theory of Communication.* Urbana: University of Illinois Press, 1949.
Siegert, Bernhard. *Relays: Literature as an Epoch of the Postal System.* Stanford, Calif.: Stanford University Press, 1999.
Standage, Tom. *The Victorian Internet: The Remarkable Story of the Telegraph and the Nineteenth Century's On-line Pioneers.* New York: Walker and Co., 1998.
Stendhal. *Lucien Leuwen.* Ed. Henri Debray and Michel Crouzet. Garnier-Flammarion 350–51. Paris: Flammarion, 1982.
———. *Lucien Leuwen. Romans et nouvelles.* Ed. Henri Martineau. Bibliothèque de la Pléiade. Paris: Gallimard, 1952. 1:731–1384.
———. *Le Rouge et le noir. Romans et nouvelles.* Ed. Henri Martineau. Bibliothèque de la Pléiade. Paris: Gallimard, 1952. 1:193–730.
———. *La Vie de Henri Brulard. Oeuvres intimes.* Ed. Henri Martineau. Bibliothèque de la Pléiade. Paris: Gallimard, 1955. 1–398.
Stengers, Isabelle. "Le Pouvoir des concepts." In *Les Concepts scientifiques.* Ed. Judith Schalnger and Isabelle Stengers. Paris: Gallimard, 1991. 29–66.
Studeny, Christophe. *L'Invention de la vitesse: France, XVIIe–XIXe siècle.* Paris: Gallimard, 1995.
Vaillé, Eugène. *Le Cabinet noir.* Paris: PUF, 1950.
———. *Histoire des postes depuis la Révolution.* Paris: PUF, 1947.
Vale, Edmund. *The Mail-Coach Men of the Late Eighteenth Century.* London: Cassell, 1960.
Virilio, Paul. *Bunker Archeology.* New York: Princeton Architectural Press, 1994.
———. *Guerre et cinéma I: Logistique de la perception.* Paris: Éditions Cahiers du cinéma, 1991.
———. *L'Horizon négatif: Essai de dromologie.* Paris: Galilée, 1984.
———. *L'Insécurité du territoire.* Paris: Galilée, 1993.

———. *Vitesse et politique.* Paris: Galilée, 1977.

Wiener, Norbert. *Cybernetics or Control and Communication in the Animal and the Machine.* Cambridge, Mass.: M.I.T. Press, 1948.

Wilson, Geoffrey. *The Old Telegraphs.* London: Phillimore, 1976.

Winthrop-Young, Geoffrey. "The Informatics of Revenge: Speed and Storage in *The Count of Monte Cristo.*" *Weber Studies: An Interdisciplinary Humanities Journal* 14.1 (Winter 1997). <http://www.altx.com/ebr/w(ebr)/essays/wyoung.html> (February 6, 2000).

Zola, Émile. *La Bête humaine. Les Rougon-Macquart.* Ed. Henri Mitterand. Bibliothèque de la Pléiade. Paris: Gallimard, 1966. 995–1331.

INDEX

DAVID F. BELL is a professor of French at Duke University. He is the author of *Models of Power: Politics and Economics in Zola's "Rougon-Macquart"* (1988) and *Circumstances: Chance in the Literary Text* (1993), a coeditor of *Hermes: Literature, Philosophy, Science* (1982), and the editor and translator of *Joyful Cruelty: Toward a Philosophy of the Real* (1993).

The University of Illinois Press
is a founding member of the
Association of American University Presses.

Composed in 9.5/12.5 Trump Mediaeval
by Jim Proefrock
at the University of Illinois Press
Manufactured by Thomson-Shore, Inc.

University of Illinois Press
1325 South Oak Street
Champaign, IL 61820-6903
www.press.uillinois.edu